W9-CQC-668

DREAMING AT THE CROSSROADS OF CHANGE

by Linda Kavelin-Popov

Dreaming at the Crossroads of Change

Copyright © Linda Kavelin-Popov 2020

All rights reserved

This book may be purchased at Amazon.com

For information on Linda Kavelin-Popov's other books and blog, visit

www.lindakavelinpopov.com

Cover photo and design, interior design by Dan Popov, Ph.D.

LIBRARY OF CONGRESS CATALOGUING IN-PUBLICATION DATA

Popov, Linda Kavelin; Kavelin-Popov, Linda; virtues; retirement; inspiration; self-help; future; grief

Dreaming at the Crossroads of Change; change management; Virtues Project.

No part of this book may be reproduced or transmitted in any form or by any means, electronic or mechanical, including photocopying or recording without permission in writing from the author.

ISBN 9798570573796

Printed in the United States

Dedication

To the memory of my fierce and faithful She-Bear sister, Cheryll Simmons, whose courage at her crossroads inspired this book.

TABLE OF CONTENTS

Introduction

Change at any season in our lives holds great promise. Something new is about to unfold. It brings with it both trepidation and hope. Will we be thrust onto a perilous trail of unknowns, plunging us into anxiety, or is it going to be a grand adventure? The way we choose to respond to change makes all the difference.

How do we manage radical change while staying sane, and transform a time of stress into a mindful pause to contemplate our truest dreams? *Dreaming at the Crossroads* is a guide to navigating the major shifts in your life, by calling on the power of virtues – your inner qualities of soul and character. Simple strategies sourced in these spiritual powers can help you discern a path which, in your heart of hearts, you really want to take.

A loss, a move, retirement, graduation, or even a crisis opens a whole new world before us. Great courage is required to face the unknowns these changes bring and to mine their gifts. We need to trust that we will not only survive but thrive, if we make creative and sustainable choices.

How do we entertain the possibility of bringing a new dream to life? How do we begin to envision it? Sometimes even profound grief can shift us into a new perception of what we want at this season. You may feel lost and bereft, or excited, but without guideposts. As co-founder of The Virtues Project, I believe that the time-honored virtues, such as love, justice, compassion, and gratitude, are the interior tools we need to succeed in any situation. Virtues are universally valued positive qualities of character, described in the diverse faiths and wisdom sources of the world as the purpose of life, the qualities of the soul, and the "fruits of the spirit." They are personal practices that enable us to tap into a power we may not have realized we possess, one sourced in the essence of who we are.

"I Wisdom am mistress of discretion, inventor of lucidity of thought."

Proverbs 8:11 – 12

The intent of this book is to illuminate a way forward as you ride the waves of change, by helping you tap into your innate wisdom. May the virtues strategies described here be a wellspring of support as you create your own unique dream and discern your true intentions.

This is meant to be a contemplative experience. Each chapter contains exercises inviting you to practice reflection and open to your imagination, by taking a compassionate and honest look at your inner thoughts, feelings and hopes. A journal would be a helpful companion as you reflect.

If you're recovering from a loss, making a move, seeking a new livelihood, facing retirement, or coping with major changes in your lifestyle, my hope is that this book will help you to discern your dream and bring it to life.

CHAPTER ONE

THE COURAGE TO CHOOSE CHANGE

"Change is the egg of the phoenix."

Christina Baldwin, author, *Calling the Circle*

Whenever we reach a major crossroads in life, the necessity to choose how or where to live faces us full on. Shifting out of our normal work, lifestyle, or study patterns is a kind of leaving home, whether literally or emotionally. Our roles have largely defined us, and our days have been filled by these activities. When a role changes, the abundance of both uncertainties and possibilities can seem overwhelming. Some have described it as "staring into an abyss", "a grand canyon of possibilities", or "jumping off the edge of the known world."

You may feel discontent with your current lifestyle, and long for a change. Does your regular life feel stale, boring, too overwhelming or demanding? Even if the status quo brings a measure of pleasure, are the aspects you don't like starting to wear down your enthusiasm? Physical, or emotional fatigue is a strong signal from your spirit that it's time for something new, or at least a sabbatical into a fresh perspective. Whatever the change occurring in your life, it may be time to consider opening to new freedom.

Cheryll's Story: Embracing her Freedom Season

Every summer for a decade, ten women gathered at a small lodge on the Koksilah River on Vancouver Island, off the West Coast of Canada for a week of floating, swimming, singing, crafting, praying, and sharing our lives. We moved the retreat to Lake Chelan in Eastern Washington for another ten years. We named ourselves the She-Bears, and have fiercely guarded each other's backs and served as one another's story-keepers to this day, even though we live in different countries.

When Cheryll was facing the terrifying prospect of retiring from her beloved job as a family advocate at a social services agency, she asked me to meet her for a private retreat – just the two of us – at a Bed and Breakfast tucked into a forest in Washington State.

As we walked beside a gently burbling river, she poured out her heart. "Who will I be without my work? What will I do every day?" Her younger partner, a concert cellist and music teacher, had years of work ahead of her, so Cheryll knew her days would loom with a daunting amount of solitude once she took the unimaginable step into retirement. She was deeply invested in supporting the underprivileged families she served with her powerful sense of justice. Her identity was fully entwined with her work. Yet, encroaching aging, which involved a good bit of pain, forced her to recognize that it was time to let go.

One evening, as we labored and laughed over a crossword puzzle, she said, "I just hate that word 'retirement'. Sounds like a useless old nag being put out to pasture."

"Hmm," I said. "Why don't we come up with another name for it?"

Cheryll looked pensive and expectant. Suddenly, a phrase appeared in my mind. "Cher, this isn't your retirement. It's your freedom season!" Her face lit up in a huge smile.

Within the year, Cheryll summoned the courage to leave her job, to set out on an unfamiliar path into an unknown season. For a few months, she tentatively explored new ways to spend her time. She read voraciously, rode a three-wheel bike around the neighborhood, and went to "clay camp" to deepen her knowledge of "caning" and other techniques for sculpting jewelry and other small objects. She launched into dedicated crafting, which she had always enjoyed. After our retreat she had taken me to a craft and bead shop, practically salivating with glee as she filled her basket with multi-colored beads, Fimo modeling clay, hooks for earrings, and chains for necklaces. Leaving her job also gave her the time to travel – always by car or train, never by plane – to visit her ailing mother in California. She and her partner, Kara, drove up from Washington State to British Columbia where Dan and I were tending my beloved brother, John, as he was dying of brain cancer. On John's last night, he was exquisitely serenaded by Kara on cello. When Kara and Cher left to spend the night at a local hotel, he said, "It doesn't get any better than this." He had his final seizure the next morning, and Cheryll and Kara were there to hold me before he died.

In 2016, Cheryll was diagnosed with pancreatic cancer. She sought every possible cure, but in February of 2017, she passed. Cher was the first of the ten She-Bears to die. She lived fully for the few years of her retirement, seeking out like-minded crafters, sharing her creations with friends, and relishing her freedom every single day.

Know when to cut your losses

If, like Cheryll, you're on the brink of retirement, it may seem as if the word "freedom" obscures something quite frightening – a downshift, an unmooring, as if you are being set adrift into an unknown, structure-less world, where you have no clear idea how to spend your days. Better to make the shift consciously than to give in to lethargy, binge watching, or endless golf. Questions arise like yeast in bread. What will give you daily meaning? Who will you be? What will you do? What is your reason to get up in the morning? A crisis such as illness, loss, or a divorce also forces us to reconsider our priorities. A move forces us to completely reorient to a new space, new people, new streets and services, to let go of the familiar and step out of our comfort zone. Courage calls us to tap into our imaginations, to envision new possibilities based on our tastes, our needs, our wants, and our gifts. To do that, we need to reflect deeply. Who am I at this stage in my life? What do I truly care about? What are the limitations I need to accept that circumscribe my choices?

"Every set-back is a set-up for a come-back."

Tony Robbins, author, *The Power to Shape Your Destiny*

Kevin and Pam's Story: Necessity is the Mother of Reinvention

For thirty years, this New Zealand couple worked a dairy farm and raised a family side by side, without any hired labor. They "could read each other's thoughts" and most days, worked together seamlessly. "Pam was the brains, I was the brawn," said Kevin. During calving season in July, they worked from 4:30 am to 6 pm, then collapsed. And they had three children at home as well. Life was tied to the seasons, and the rhythms of their lives varied accordingly. They were deeply connected to the farming community, hosting many a barbecue or buffet to celebrate the end of calving or haying time. "We all worked hard and played hard," said Kevin.

In his early fifties, Kevin needed dual hip replacements. As he was recovering from surgery, he began to feel more and more ill, and later discovered that he was allergic to the titanium balls that had been inserted into his hips. He was bed ridden much of the time, unable to be the active man he had been, reduced to doing only simple chores. As he became increasingly depressed and irritable, Pam said, "I felt really helpless and very much alone." Pam revealed that this had been a painful test of their relationship, and she was at a loss to know how to retrieve their closeness and a modicum of the contented life that now seemed to be over. Then, Kevin twisted an ankle while milking, and that ended the life he loved as a farmer. His doctor told him he must never again put on a pair of gumboots. As he and Pam walked out of the doctor's office, they looked at each other and said, "Let's sell the farm."

Their decisiveness led to a major shift to a more town-oriented lifestyle and eventually, to new work that brings each of them joy – Kevin as a driver of disabled children and youth, and Pam as a teacher. Kevin now delights in bringing smiles to the faces of his young passengers. Looking back, Kevin believes that their courage to make a swift decision may have saved him years of depression, watching a hired man do what he was helpless to do any longer on his beloved farm. There is much they miss about their old lifestyle, especially the close-knit farming community. They're creating smaller social circles now and realize that the choice they made gave them a new, albeit different, lease on life. Instead of growing crops, they're now nurturing young souls.

Anything is possible, even in disaster, if we have the courage and creativity to find a new way forward. Yes, radical change in health or circumstances forces us out of our comfort zone. It's a true stretch, and we need to believe that we have the strength to find our resilience.

Freeing yourself from your regular role may feel like an unfathomable sacrifice. Sacrifice isn't just about giving up a dream. It's creating space for a new dream, one that fits your life now. The true meaning of sacrifice is "to make sacred" – to treat your life with reverence. It requires trust in the journey itself, including its turns and shifts in direction. Choosing to consciously practice the virtues of courage and trust actually magnetizes opportunities.

"If plan A fails, remember you have twenty-five letters left."

Henry W. Guest, author

Dare to Discern

Are you willing to open to the possibility of change? Then, yes, you're taking a huge risk – that everything will feel new, that you may experience unaccustomed joy and actually reinvent yourself. Initiating a new path in your life brings a smorgasbord of choices – new ways to live, serve, and play.

Even if you remain in your current role, or you run your own business, yet still sense it's time for a change of direction, you have every right to consider a new way to live your life. You have far more freedom than you may realize, even when the realities of your life seem circumscribed. It's time to get real and take a long, compassionate and honest look at your feelings and the facts of your life.

It takes courage to lean trustingly into a new season, ready to turn a fresh page. Discernment is needed to envision a restorative, stimulating, sustainable life. It takes optimism to forge a path to a new dream.

Reflection Exercise 1: Taking Stock

Before you step off the cliff of your known life, unsure whether you will fall or fly, take some time away from the familiar to reflect on this looming change. To contemplate a new normal, you first need to assess your situation. Keep a journal or tablet with you to record your thoughts. Go somewhere you will feel nurtured and free of responsibilities. The guest room of a friend. A cabin in the forest. A seashore bungalow. A road trip. Somewhere you can walk, sit and gaze, smell new scents, and experience the novelty of silence, relieved of daily demands. Even a few days of uninterrupted quiet can open your mind to new guidance.

Assess your current situation. With an attitude of openness and honesty, ask yourself

- How am I, really?
- What drains me?
- What sustains me?
- What do I want less of in my life at this season?
- What feelings do I have about this possible change?

"Worry does not empty tomorrow of its sorrow; it empties today of its strength."

Corrie Ten Boom, Dutch author

Dive deeper. Drag your worries out of the lurking dark. Examine them with compassion and detachment, free of judgment. Feelings don't respond to shoulds or shouldn'ts. They simply are. When examined, they lose their gravitas.

- What do I fear about leaving my role? (or my city, or this lifestyle)

- What is the hardest thing to give up? Is it an idea of success not yet reached? Is it guilt at giving up a long held responsibility? A goal unachieved? The familiarity of my current routine?
- How do I normally respond to change?
- What do I need in order to feel safe as I make a shift from my normal work and life? A certain amount of savings? Time with friends or family?

Once you have given yourself time and space to reflect on those questions, **focus on the future**:

- What do I want to stop doing, keep doing, and start doing for the life I truly want? (Take your time on this one.)
- What would restorative rest look like to me? Is that what I need first?
- What adventures excite me?
- What do I want more of in my life?
- What lifestyle appeals to me?
- Is some new purpose calling to me?

A friend once said, "I don't know what I think until I say it." If you are someone who gains clarity from talking things out, find someone you trust, have them ask you these questions, and share your reflections with them. You don't need someone else's wisdom right now. You only need your own truth and courage to fully explore life's invitations.

CHAPTER TWO

GRIEF AS A CATALYST FOR HOPE

"There is a crack in everything. That's how the light gets in."

Leonard Cohen, Canadian poet, composer, and singer

Change brings grief in its wake. Loss of the familiar, with the comfort of the well-known, well-trodden paths we are used to, even if we are less than happy in those ruts, is a daunting experience. If we love the life we've been living and suddenly lose it, whatever change has occurred, grief descends without our permission.

Opening to hope for a new dream of what is possible – one we truly want – requires us first to acknowledge and honor our sadness, and hear our own sorrow. If we process it patiently, grief can heal us. It will scour us out and prepare us for fresh possibilities. It is hard to believe that and we certainly don't want to hear it when we're in the midst of fresh loss. (Especially from well-meaning friends or family intent on rushing us past this seismic shift in our souls!) Yet, the time will come when we know we have to move on.

"People coming out of calamity are open to sweeping changes."

Margaret MacMullan, Toronto professor quoted in The Economist, May 9, 2020

Move through Grief like a Whale

We may find ourselves grieving on many levels – the loss of our normal lives, and perhaps the many things that need changing in our world. We cannot ignore our grief, or it will literally make us sick. We need to befriend it. I wrote a great deal about this in my book, *Graceful Endings*: Navigating the Journey of Loss and Grief. Yet, a book about new dreams at a turning point of change would be remiss not to mention that grief is a significant aspect of awakening to the new. It's the mulch for the garden, the soil for new growth.

The healthiest process for dealing with stressful feelings, in my experience as a psychotherapist, spiritual care director at hospice, and in my own life, is to respond like a whale. Whales plunge into the depths of the sea, then come up for air, and even breach the water, leaping high. We need to create safe spaces to experience the depths of our grief, diving right down into it, ideally with a compassionate witness to companion us, who will not resist or judge our tears or our anger. Some need to be alone to release their pain, either in their car or on a deserted trail or beach.

Then, we need to come up for air, engage in something that would give us pleasure, such as a run, a video, a game, a good novel, a conversation with someone we enjoy, or crafting something beautiful. Bring your attention to your feelings, then detach. Dive deep into them, then come up, dive and come up for air. This dance of compassion and detachment is an effective method to avoid stuffing feelings down with food, alcohol or drugs, becoming physically ill from suppressing them, giving into rage attacks, or breaking down completely.

In my work as a psychotherapist and grief counselor in community mental health centers and in healing retreats among First Nations, I specialized in suicide prevention, among teens and adults. Successful intervention in supporting people in drug and alcohol treatment centers, tribal gatherings, and prisons to move forward positively with their lives involved first inviting them to vent their grief fully – and loudly – and then to refocus on committing to their own happiness.

What helped them to move forward was being in the safe space of a Virtues Healing Circle (See Resources), sharing their stories in the presence of receptive silence, venting their emotions without advice, interruption, or judgments, then being honored for their virtues by others in the circle. They would also do Virtues Picks, giving them a simple practice to guide their healing journey. This powerful process has brought many toughened, scarred souls into floods of healing tears, open to the embraces of their peers.

The whale dance of diving deep, emptying their cup of pain, then being restored with virtues acknowledgments, enabled them to rise to a new challenge. They were able to call on their courage, creativity, and service to others to build a new way forward.

Johnny's Story: Healing the Past: Creating Hope for the Future

A dozen men were ordered into a van by their village chief and sent to a lodge on the Alaska Highway to meet with me, a random white woman they had never heard of or met. Unbeknownst to me, the chief did nothing to prepare them. When he first walked into the trailer where I was facilitating the healing circle, Johnny took one look at me and swore. "I'm not staying in this f---ing place!" Yet he filed in with the others and took a seat, mumbling the whole time. I briefly introduced myself, and gave a short description of a virtues healing circle and set the boundaries: the need to listen in receptive silence to each person's turn, to put on a shield of compassion and detachment while listening, and to use the virtues poster to honor each man when he finished. It was met with a deathly silence. I then turned to Johnny, and asked, "What's your name?"

"Johnny."

"Johnny, what is it about staying in this f---ing place?"

"I hate white people!" he roared.

Matching his tone, I yelled, "What do you hate?" and pulled my chair across from him.

Johnny poured out his story of being stolen from his village at five years old and placed in a religious residential school. His hair was cut, his name and language were taken, and he was kept from seeing his family for months. And on and on.

By the time he finished, we were all in tears, as was Johnny.

I gave him his first virtues acknowledgment. "Johnny, I honor you for your courage to speak the truth."

One by one, the men honored his courage, his strength and other virtues. He lit up in a huge smile and said, "I'm staying!" He became my shadow for the rest of the week-long retreat and begged me to move to his community. From that point on, whenever he learned that I was in the Yukon, he tracked me down, and brought a moose he had shot, or some other gift to whatever workshop I was giving.

Find the Humor

Humor is also part of the process of healthy grieving. Humor was the guiding light in a private session with an eighty-six year old woman, afflicted both by dementia and terminal cancer. At the start of the session, she cheerily said, "You know, I won't remember a thing afterwards. That's why I'm recording it." We both chuckled over that. Once she began to trust me, she blushed deeply, and whispered conspiratorially, that she secretly believed in the goddess. We were meeting in a convent counseling room, and her family were all Catholic! So, for the rest of our session, I would say, "Thank Goddess, you can still walk!" or similar things. She found this hilarious. At the close of the session, she told me she hadn't laughed so much in years.

Use Loss as Grist for Transformation

Radical change – even profound loss – can lead us to a new dream. When we lose our normal bearings and coordinates, we receive the opportunity to plot a new course. It cannot be rushed, and the timing is highly personal.

I have experienced the uniqueness of this timing myself. My younger brother John was my close companion and friend all of our lives. He was a gifted Imagineer for Walt Disney and left that role to collaborate with me and my husband, Dan, on an initiative called The Virtues Project, which grew into a global grassroots movement in more than 100 countries. We lived and worked together and traveled the world sharing the Project for two decades until John contracted terminal brain cancer. Dan and I cancelled months of speaking engagements to care for him until his death. Afterwards, I was devastated by the vast hole left in my brother's wake.

The first year without John was shockingly painful. Yet it brought with it a transformative change building below the ground of my conscious life. Dan and I flew off for a recovery holiday to a gorgeous little island in the South Pacific named Aitutaki, in the Cook Islands, where we had been invited several times before to present The Virtues Project. It was there, gazing at the turquoise lagoon that I began to come back to myself, and found healing in creativity. I began writing *Graceful Endings,* which recounts what I learned about giving John a graceful end of life and what I and others need, to navigate the grief afterwards.

The following year, Dan, and I were having the conversation, "Where would you go if I die before you?" I said I would finally stay put on Salt Spring Island in British Columbia, Canada, settle into writing and become a dedicated lunchist with my friends. We had traveled the world for more than twenty years speaking on virtues, and rarely had much time at home, so I was ready to roost.

Dan's answer was totally different: "Oh, I'd go to Aitutaki," he said.

"What? Of all the places in the world, why would you go to that tiny, remote island?" I asked.

"The beauty… and there's something about the people," he said.

Later that evening, he came to me and said, "You know, I would so, so, so much rather go there *with* you." I tossed and turned, wakeful throughout the night. Then, the inner voice of guidance spoke, loud and clear: "It's his turn." For twenty-five years, Dan had remained with me on Salt Spring Island, despite his restless need to move. The next morning, as we sat in our recliners looking out at the view of forest, sea and mountains, I said, "Okay."

"Okay, what?"

"Okay, let's go to Aitutaki."

Three weeks after the decision was made, our house was empty, ready to be put on the market, our worldly goods sold or given away, and we took off. After we arrived on Aitutaki, staying in a guest house on the beach, we gave ourselves six weeks to make the decision whether to settle there. A local friend asked us to listen to a demo of her new CD, with island songs and stories. One of them was about how Aitutaki got its name. Polynesian voyagers were seeking a new home and were tossed mercilessly in a violent storm, waves threatening to swamp them. They prayed to Tangaroa, god of the sea and Rangi, god of the sky, to save them. When they landed safely on the shores of a small island, they named it Aitutaki – "guided by the hands of the gods." Hearing that was a confirmation that we had been guided here, and that indeed, this was home.

During the six years we remained on Aitutaki, we made lasting friendships. We were virtually adopted by a Cook Islands Maori family, and helped to raise a two year old named Alii Tasi Renata Fepulaeai. She called us Mama and Papa, the island term for grandparents. Several friends offered to bury us in their yards when our time came – a rare honor. We expected to remain in the Cook Islands for the rest of our lives, but in late 2018, immigration changes affecting Americans and other ex-pats compelled us to leave.

We were forced into a change we never expected, and the scene at the airport was heart-breaking. People were crying and putting leis around our necks, and our granddaughter looked up at me sadly, as if to say, "How can you leave me, Mama?" I was gutted. The departing tourists must have wondered what was going on. Once more, I was plunged into profound grief for the dissolution of the life we had planned.

When we left, we had no certainty about where we would live, but only a simple transition plan. Not wanting to leave Polynesia, we returned to our home country of the U.S., to the state of Hawaii. We decided to explore several islands, beginning with Lanai, one of the smaller Hawaiian Islands. We never left, and this change, forced though it was, has led us home once again.

I learned that even a painful change, suddenly and unintentionally imposed on us, enveloping us in unknowns, can lead to a new dream, if we follow the path that flows from virtues, such as trust, decisiveness, and courage.

Life in Hawaii is more first-world than Aitutaki, with far better medical care, and even access to Costco on the neighboring island of Maui. There are many kind, fascinating people here, and a fresh aspect of beauty, with Lanai's stately Cook Islands Pines (another connection), mountains and seascapes. Within the first year, we have made close friends, and once again have island children in our lives. I grieved the loss of our life in Aitutaki deeply for the first several months, but thanks to technology, we still see and talk with our Tasi and the rest of our Cook Islands family.

For us, leaping into unknown adventures has allowed us to live the dream. Others' ideas of the good life vary greatly. Island living isn't for everyone. What matters is giving oneself permission to dream.

The remaining chapters in *Dreaming at the Crossroads* offer a way for you to reset your own life with hope, optimism, and even joy.

"To 'listen' another's soul into a condition of disclosure and self-discovery may be almost the greatest service any human being ever performs for another."

Douglas Van Steere, American Quaker theologian

Reflection Exercise 2: Befriend Your Grief

- Journal about a loss or grief you are experiencing now. Describe where you feel it in your body, and what effect it is having on you. Use words or drawings.

- Identify someone trustworthy with whom you feel safe sharing this – either a counselor, friend or family member who is a good listener. Release your emotions as freely as you can.

- Journal and share what is your hope in this situation and how you can sustain your hope in the midst of testing times?

- Think of someone who could use your listening ear and reach out to them. Offer them your attentive presence. Put on a shield of compassion and detachment so you can be fully present without taking on their feelings. When they finish sharing, give them a virtues acknowledgment. "I see your courage to move through this." "Thank you for your trust to share with me." (See Resources for Spiritual Companioning Steps).

CHAPTER THREE

TRUST THE PROCESS

"As soon as you trust yourself, you will know how to live."

Johann Wolfgang von Goethe, German philosopher

As you unravel the knots of doubt and call on the courage to make a change, you are actually letting go of your known life. Now what? For some, this early phase of standing at a crossroads can be quite frightening. You're in totally unfamiliar territory.

First of all, realize you cannot rush the process. You have to trust it. It will have its own timing and its particular rhythm. Trust yourself to sort it out, but understand that it may not happen quickly. If you are like most people, you probably don't have a detailed, ready-made plan for change. The truth is, you don't need one. In fact, it would be a preemptive strike against Grace to do so. With each step you take, new vistas will open.

"Take the first step in faith. You don't have to see the whole staircase. Just take the first step."
Dr. Martin Luther King, Jr.

Step onto the bridge

Most of us aren't ready to map out our entire lives for a new season. What we do need, in order to prevent the sheer terror of "nothing to do now" from swallowing us whole, is to take a single step – namely to create a gentle transition plan.

Your transition plan is not meant to establish a long-term vision for how you'll spend the rest of your life. At the moment, you need a simple way to bridge the divide between your former way of life and your future. When leaving your paid work or any long-term role, dissolving a relationship, moving to a new place, or saying goodbye when your youngest child leaves the nest, give yourself breathing space – gentle time to gather possibilities.

Take a Holy Pause

The ultimate purpose of a pause when you are at a crossroads is to enter into deep discernment about a new direction. Call on the patience to give yourself a waiting period before committing to any particular course. The exception to this is when the fates put a decision before you that must be made by a definite time, and the date is fast approaching. As daunting as this can feel, you still need to slow your mind down into deep contemplation rather than letting it career about like a ping pong ball in a tile bathroom. The goal is not to be impulsive but decisive.

Sometimes a choice appears, and we must make it immediately, prompted by a deep knowing that it is right and timely. To be able to trust that kind of instinct you need to gentle your mind and take the space to reflect, not just fling ideas around, but true down into what really matters to you. Write things down, ask the right questions, and sink into your inner wisdom. Ask your angels and guides. Trust your inner knowing. Logic alone is not enough when making life-changing decisions. Even small decision such as how to spend one's day will vary if we tap into the wellspring of deeper knowledge. I have often found that if I ask for guidance about where I am meant to be today to be of service, a face will come into my mind, even of someone I hardly know, and when I go to where they are, they say something like, "Thank God you came."

When you have the luxury of ample time to discern a new way forward, it's best to hold decisions lightly with patience, prayer and deep contemplation. Don't attempt to refill your life right away with activities, except those that arise in your mind with gentle immediacy, such as meeting a friend for coffee. Don't overfill your time. Savor the silence and solitude. Find a temporary balance, with time to reflect, to move, to play, and to reach out to people. Do things you've wanted to do but haven't had the time. Read one of the books on your wish list. Design a pleasurable day. Take the hike you've been too busy for and call someone fun to accompany you.

"The harder you work, the harder it is to surrender."

Vince Lombardi, Super Bowl winning coach

Rachel's Story: The Power to Change Her Mind

Six months before her third and final attempt to retire from a job of more than twenty-five years as director of a Family Treatment Center for recovering alcoholics and addicts, Rachel told me, "Having so many choices is both a great freedom and a daunting weight. I have so many 'want-tos' for when I retire that I have to shut my mind off." She decided to talk to her therapist about it, who said not to make any major moves for a year after she retired. "I was vastly relieved by this." One of Rachel's challenges was that her colleagues and employees had become her social circle and were truly like family. Letting go of her role felt like choosing to be homeless.

Rachel's path took an unexpected turn after she decided to move back to wintery Alberta, Canada where some family members lived. She rented a condo in a new building. After several months of bone-numbing, often sub-zero temperatures, she longed once again for the more temperate climate of her former home, and the warmth of her colleagues – her chosen family. She accepted a part- time consultancy contract with the treatment center, and happily moved back to Vancouver Island off Canada's west coast to stay. That would serve as her base for travel to warmer places during the winter, including visiting my husband and me in Hawaii. I told Rachel that her decision reminded me of the story of the Bluebird of Happiness. It was in her own backyard all the time.

Learn the quiet joy of single-pointed attention. Give up multi-tasking for the moment, even if going on all cylinders is your habitual and preferred way to operate. It may be uncomfortable at first. Let it be what it is.

"Gardening is a natural anti-depressant. It gives you a stake in the future."

Linda Gillard, author, *House of Silence*

Stop and smell the roses – literally. If you have a garden, spend some quality time there. It is an indigenous teaching that if you plant your bare feet on the ground, you are literally anchoring on the earth, grounding your soul. If you plunge your bare hands into soil, it is said to be a natural healer, relieving anxiety and depression. Whether or not this has been proven scientifically, it feels really good. Let the scents of mint, sage, or rose penetrate your awareness. If you happen to be awake at dawn, get up and take in the soft waking of the world. If you have a kitchen garden in a city apartment, pull off a piece of mint or rosemary, rub it between your fingers and take a deep whiff.

The timeless feeling of gardening gently restores mind and spirit.

Don't succumb to the haunting belief that to extract the meaning of your existence, you have to catch up on all the chores you've put off because you've been too busy, reorganize your home office, or launch a new career in volunteering. It's premature to launch anything! Don't rush into activity to alleviate anxiety about the thunderous sound of silence or guilt about losing your "usefulness". Take a breath. Savor your morning cup. Dare to stare and putter, walk and meander. Be aimless for a while.

"There is certainly something in angling that tends to produce a serenity of mind."

Washington Irving, American author

Go fishing, which, by the way, is not the same thing as catching. It's about the beauty of the water, the sheer mindless (some would say mindful) joy of rewinding and casting your line. The quiet. Thinking is optional, but best left aside. Watching my husband gracefully casting his fly rod at a trout stream was a breathtaking experience of Grace. For him, it has been a meditation. I have a regular rod, and for me, just casting and rewinding completely engages my mind and detaches me from thought. A rare gift.

Take a Personal Retreat

When I have needed a break from normal life, or had a decision to make, I have often taken a private retreat for a few days somewhere peaceful, such as a convent, where meals were provided, there were trails to walk, a garden to sit in, and sometimes a labyrinth. Comfortable clothes, a journal, my virtues cards, my water bottle, and a good novel are my only provisions. A journal can be a canvass for writing, drawing, or making mandalas. During such small sabbaticals, silence opens up a sacred space for reflection.

Sleep, Perchance to Dream

Some people need to sleep in order to discover a new dream. You can choose to sleep in your own bed, on an island far from home, or a cabin in the forest. Give yourself full permission to nap. It doesn't mean you're putting yourself out to pasture. It's a source of renewal and strength.

"Naps are the adult version of a child's fort. A love of privacy and a place for make-believe. Rest adds strength to our souls."

Sark, American author

Pursue the perfect nap. Proactive rest is best – resting before you get tired, usually about six or seven hours after waking. Whatever you do, don't get entrapped and numb yourself by endless hours as a couch potato watching television, playing games on your smartphone, or reacting to constant prompts from social media. According to the Netflix documentary, "The Social Dilemma", we are all subject to massive manipulation by our social media platforms which have made them as addictive as possible and have us checking for "likes" or tweets or texts multiple times a day. A little bit of screen time can be good for you. A lot is deadening and distracts you from living.

Expose Yourself to Beauty

Be a tourist in your own town. Search out the best foods, the loveliest views, the most interesting sights, the best walks. Wander through a farmers' market. Take a day trip and bring along a journal.

Allow your mind to wander and ponder. What do you enjoy? What kind of lifestyle calls to you?

Larry's Story: From High Tech to Island Living

Soon after Dan and I arrived in the Cook Islands, we met Larry, an American ex-pat who had been living on Aitutaki for fifteen years. He ended up choosing this tiny island in the South Pacific after discerning two principles to guide his final season: At the age of fifty-five, he made himself two promises: first, that he wouldn't see winter again, and second, he would never again get into a life situation where he was compelled to work for a living.

In his pre-island life, Larry was an internet technology specialist, and taught Management Information Systems for six years at a business college in Washington State. He had been married and divorced twice. He planned to start collecting Social Security at age 62 and had already acquired some retirement income. He began searching for a way to keep both his promises.

In his late forties, when he flew to French Polynesia, people kept mentioning the neighboring Cook Islands in the South Pacific as a beautiful,

44

non-touristy place. Two years later, he read about Aitutaki in Lonely Planet *and spent several weeks there. He contacted Araura College, learned they were desperate for supplies, went back to Spokane, and contacted a high school with a Sister School program. When he returned to Aitutaki a few months later, he had packed a few of his earthly belongings in a container, including a massive number of books, along with ample computers and school supplies. He volunteered to teach computer skills at the high school, and was the first computer teacher on the island. He's been in Aitutaki ever since and last I heard, he serves occasionally as a substitute teacher. Otherwise his time is his own. .*

When people ask him what he's been doing lately, he says, with a grin of satisfaction, "Very little." He's a self-confessed gourmand "foodie" and has a well-developed knack for foraging through the small island shops for Brie and Camembert, black olives, multi-grain mustard, and good bread. Yet Larry does have one other passion. He enthusiastically offers free tours to visitors, showing them the highlights of the island. "I love showing off our island," he says. Larry says, "Retirement is a state of mind, not a state of income." Larry took his time to discern his dream,

and now he's living it. He has found true
contentment on his island Paradise. Because he
became a permanent resident in the years when
that was still on offer, he has been there for twenty
years and is able to live there for the rest of his
life.

Reflection Exercise 3: Prepare for Dreaming

- Consider what would allow you to have a
  real rest, a genuine pause to clear your mind.
  Choose one that is affordable and to which
  you have easy access. Following the passing
  of my beloved brother John fifteen months
  after we began caring for him, Dan and I
  took a trip to a lovely beachside resort on
  Aitutaki, where we did hardly anything but
  lie in a hammock, read, float in a turquoise
  lagoon, and rouse ourselves to eat a couple
  of times a day. Little did we know we would
  return to live there a couple of years later.

- Cultivate an attitude of trust – trust that your
  path will appear. The world will be your
  oyster, with or without ample funds. There
  are plenty of crafts to pursue, culinary dishes
  to create, people who need companionship,
  services to offer, and countless ways to play.

New remote jobs are cropping up continually and some fields of work are expanding greatly with work from home options.

- Take time to envision your ideal lifestyle. Then reflect on steps you can take to make it real. What have you always wanted to do but never had the time for before? Read, travel, write a book, sort all your photos, build something, clean out the attic, take up golf, start a small business? If you are pursuing a new livelihood, expand your thinking. Let your hopes run wild. You may well come up with your ideal job.

- Create a ritual for your transition: a party, a blessing ceremony, a planned pleasure. You may want to share your vision with friends and family. This could also be a time for a "give-away," which is a First Nations ritual at times of transition, when roles or circumstances change. Pass on treasures you have loved, but are willing to part with, and give one to each of your closest friends and family along with a note about what you appreciate about each of them – what they mean to you. I did this for my fiftieth birthday and found it to be a sacrificial yet invigorating release.

- Whatever you do, avoid isolating, or spending excessive time staring at a screen. Open yourself to beauty, adventure, friendship, and service. There is surprising joy in discovering how much you receive when you give of your time – far more than the act of service itself. It also opens you to a sense of community found nowhere else.

Above all, trust the process. Learn to flow with this moment of change in your life. As Bruce Lee, actor and martial artist said, "Be water, my friend."

As you examine the elements of your life, meditate on Jalal'u'din Rumi's poem:

The Guest House

This being human is a guest house.
Every morning a new arrival.

A joy, a depression, a meanness,
some momentary awareness comes
as an unexpected visitor.

Welcome and entertain them all!
Even if they are a crowd of sorrows,
who violently sweep your house
empty of its furniture,
still, treat each guest honorably.
He may be clearing you out
for some new delight.

The dark thought, the shame, the malice.
Meet them at the door laughing and invite them in.

Be grateful for whatever comes
because each has been sent
as a guide from beyond.

CHAPTER FOUR

DARE TO DREAM

"The biggest adventure you can ever take is to live the life of your dreams."

Oprah Winfrey

Entertain Idealism

Idealism is the ability to dream – to imagine what is possible, for a better world, and a better life – and to make the ideal real. Whatever your circumstances, you have the capacity to adapt and to manifest something new. The act of giving yourself permission to discern a new path forward is the first step toward recreating your life.

Many of us are so bound by a sense of hyper-responsibility that we find it a puzzling challenge to relax the habit of a pressuring ourselves to get it all done. For some, keeping busy all the time is actually a way to stay out of our feeling reality. So, the risk of slowing down into mindfulness is that long tamped feelings may arise. When this occurs, it also releases seeds of joy. Daring to dream, taking the time to delve into ourselves, whatever we come up with, is likely to awaken a more robust and deeper sense of being alive, with all its variations.

The final habit in Steven Covey's book, *7 Habits of Highly Effective People* is to "Sharpen the Saw." It involves stepping away from working harder and harder, sawing away at your responsibilities, even when the saw has become dull with over-use. It is taking intentional time for self-care, reflection and retrenching, which can well lead you, as it did Steven Covey himself, to a new path. His choice to sharpen the saw brought out the writer in him. He took a sabbatical in Hawaii and birthed his classic best-seller.

Trust that you have the imagination to come up with something new and possibly even more meaningful for this time of your life. Grace may well guide you to undiscovered paths. Whether you are drawn to a leap of faith across the globe or a simple shift to new work or pastimes that deeply satisfy you, this is your time to dream. If not now, when? Sadly, some miss out on the dream because they wait too long to tackle their bucket list.

Irv and Jackie's Story: a Dream Deferred

When I served as the first Spiritual Care Director for Hospice Victoria, Canada, I was told there was no job description. It was all on-the-job learning. My teachers were the dying, their families and the dedicated staff who cared for them. One of the people I remember well is Irv. In his mid-sixties, he was just about to retire from years in government service. He and his wife, Jackie, had planned for years to travel the world together as soon as he retired. When he was diagnosed with terminal cancer at sixty-five, their dream evaporated. Irv and Jackie confided in me that they wished they had taken early retirement or time out when they were younger to have the adventure they always planned instead of "playing it safe" to work harder and longer, to build a bigger nest egg.

Despite grieving that choice, the journey they did have took them to deeper levels of intimacy. Jackie loved to play the organ. When her birthday came that year, Irv was nearing his last days, choosing to die at home. He asked their adult son to order an organ for Jackie's gift. The day he died, she played for him as he left this world.

"I lean and loaf at my ease... observing a spear of summer grass."

Walt Whitman, American Poet

Accept Your Pace

As you establish a pace that suits your transition at this crossroads of change, let your dream unfold. If you have left your regular employment, do what you have to do to bring in survival revenue, even if it's way outside your normal skill-set, but take your time to reinvent a more permanent path forward – one that will give you true satisfaction.

If you are retiring, there's no rush, and no need to feel pressured to fill your days. In your transition you may have cultivated new rhythms – a certain amount of sleep that refreshes you without making you groggy, a preferred time to wake up, time for unhurried, unharried reflection and prayer, time to read, a long morning walk or paddle, a Sunday drive, a new activity that ignites your joy, or limitless time for puttering.

One of the questions to hold lightly as you deepen your discernment is how much time to spend in solitude and how often to be with other people. Keep noticing what is life-giving for you, and what triggers guilt, discomfort or boredom. Dare to discern your yeses, aware that you may be ready for something totally different.

If you have left the workplace behind, you now have an abundance of time. Avoid relying too heavily on your primary relationship. You don't need to spend every hour together. In fact, it enlivens the relationship to have diverse activities and interests. Pursuing your own interests allows you to have small reunions in which to share your experiences.

Whether as a parent of children who now live on their own, as a caregiver whose loved one has died, or retiring from a long held job, experiencing new freedom when departing from your primary role is like entering an empty house. The echoes can seem ominous. Take your sweet time. Savor the element of surprise. Gently repopulate your time with life-giving activities. One of my favorites when I awake before dawn is to read on my Kindle in bed, and doze for an hour or even two. It feels utterly decadent and luxurious.

"You see things; and you say 'Why?' But I dream things that never were; and I say 'Why not?'"

Drift and Dabble

Going to a book club meeting a few times doesn't mean you're committed to continue going. Say things like, "I'm here to explore." See how it feels. Learning something new such as golf, Yoga or Tai Chi may greatly enhance your quality of life. Dip a toe before you dive in. Give things a try. There's no shame in trying your hand at something before signing up for life.

There's no need to keep wearing the habitual lenses of success and failure; just open yourself to what fits and what doesn't. I heard Oprah say in an interview, "Health is the new thin," referring to her epiphany that eating a better diet is not about becoming a size that your body resists, but to nurture your body as it truly needs to be cared for.

If you're paying attention, you'll know when it's time to allow a dream to unfold, to discover what's possible. Until then, putter unapologetically, rest luxuriantly, and relax your busy mind. What will your life look like if you allow your happiest possibilities to reveal themselves?

"Let the beauty we love be what we do.

There are hundreds of ways to kneel and kiss the ground."

Jalal'u'din Rumi, Persian Sufi poet

Discern the Loves of Your Life

I believe that all of us need some way to make a contribution. Meaning is an essential aspect of genuine happiness. The pursuit of mere pleasure as one's only purpose can be soul-killing, and has often led to suicides, including by well-known, wealthy celebrities. They appear to have it all, yet joy has eluded them.

There are infinite paths to service, whether in your faith community, joining an activist group that reflects your passions, a choice to spend time with a lonely person, inviting someone new to lunch and listening to their story, or signing up for a volunteer vacation. (https://www.tripsavvy.com/volunteer-travel-for-seniors-baby-boomers)

Volunteer vacations, sometimes called "voluntours" or "service learning tours," offer the opportunity to give something back while traveling. Whatever your skills or interests, you can find a rewarding volunteer vacation experience through national and international organizations. Earthwatch expeditions take place both outdoors and inside. You may find yourself cataloguing plant specimens at the Smithsonian Institution's National Museum of Natural History in Washington, DC, or counting dolphins off the coast of the Greek island of Vonitsa.

"Invent your world. Surround yourself with people, color, sounds,

and work that nourish you."

Sark

Asking yourself who you are or wish to become at this time of change is a powerful approach to discovering your current dream. When we were living in the Cook Islands, I wrote, "I am a writer on Aitutaki. I am here to love and serve. I am open to friendship." All three of these ways of being manifested richly in my life. I had a weekly column in the Cook Islands News called "Virtues in Paradise," started a blog at www.lindakavelinpopov.com, and wrote my first novel, *A Scent of Sage.* My husband's dream was to spend time in beauty and with children. He took up sunset photography, which turned into a valued community service. His creations were posted all over the island in shops, offices, eateries, the hospital and dental clinic, and across the world as well, some in the form of posters and Virtues Cards, entitled "Sunset Meditations: Reflections on the Virtues Within," (now also known as "Resilience Virtues Cards), for which I chose the quotations and wrote the text. (See Resources) Dan also took photos at Rugby, and other sports events and family photos on occasions such as Christmas in the Park and Mother's Day, then left them in the public market for people to pick up and take home as gifts. As he walked the beach each evening, local children came running up, shouting, "Take my picture, Papa Dan!" We adopted three grandchildren who called us Mama and Papa, and were constantly surrounded by beautiful island children. The saddest part of leaving Aitutaki was leaving our adopted family behind. However, they have since moved on to New Zealand, and we stay in touch often through the wonders of technology.

Sophie's Story: Sailing New Waters

At an airport, I ran into Sophie, who had attended a Pace of Grace virtues retreat with me a few years before in New Zealand. She looked radiant, and I asked her "How are you, really?" She said, "Fabulous! I've discovered a very special way to keep my pace of grace!" She proceeded to tell me that it was actually cheaper to get on a cruise ship for months than to rent a house. She had greatly enjoyed sailing around with a friend or two, then visiting other friends briefly in various countries she wanted to experience. She took pride in "having no fixed abode" during this creative transition into retirement from business. She had rented her home furnished, which brought in continual passive income. "My only problem is a storage unit packed to the gills with years of accumulation. And I don't miss a single thing! That's what I need to tackle next," she said. "It's the only thing weighing me down."

"You got to have a dream. If you don't have a dream, how you gonna have a dream come true?"

Song "Happy Talk" from *South Pacific,* music by Rogers and Hammerstein

Reflection Exercise 4: Let your dream unfold

- Be mindful of what level of activity exhilarates and energizes you. Try a new sport, dance or discipline that releases endorphins (without spraining body parts!) Include regular, guilt-free rest in your schedule as well.

- As your dream develops, make a visual of it, either with words, clay, paint or pictures. Consider making a vision board, pasting words and pictures onto a piece of poster board. Visioning is a powerful magnet for realizing dreams.

- Journaling exercise: Write "I am..." and see what comes.

- When you feel ready to focus on possibilities, consider gathering a mastermind group to brainstorm with you.

Spend some time weeding your garden, physically and spiritually. The next chapter explores the power of releasing possessions that no longer fit your life, as well as habits that you are ready to outgrow. It's about letting go of things that no longer fit your life at this season.

CHAPTER FIVE

SET YOUR HOUSE IN ORDER

"When we clear the physical clutter from our lives, we literally make way for inspiration and 'good, orderly direction' to enter."
Julia Cameron, Canadian author

Open to Mindfulness

Envisioning a new lifestyle requires a certain mental spaciousness, and a willingness to prepare for the new. Most of us need some time to float in the unknown waters of unplanned time. We need to wallow a bit, as we gear down from the shift in our lives or our thinking.

I have found it best to gradually open to one's heart's desires, including a new way to work or serve. One helpful activity is to create a clean slate on which to mindfully examine the activities, people and places that are life-giving for you – as the person you are now, not the roles you've been playing.

This process of discerning what you want and who you want to be is nothing less than a journey of self-discovery. As a friend recently told me, "I don't want to be 'wife' or 'grandmother'. I want to be me." She had just shared in glowing terms her enjoyment of her grandchildren, and her statement had nothing to do with rejecting them. She simply wants to know herself and be known beyond expectations or the part she plays in her family. She is experiencing a higher calling to her personal identity. My longtime friend, Sister of St. Anne, Judi Morin with whom I have shared a co-spiritual director relationship for decades, said, as we entered our fifties, "We've lived fifty years from our persona. Now it's time to live from our essence." Sorting out the elements that will inhabit a new dream is a leap of faith into authentic self-expression. It is listening to the voice of your soul.

Clear the Way with Orderliness

"Have nothing in your home that you do not know to be useful

or believe to be beautiful."

William Morris, Designer

A powerful way to begin this process is by literally setting one's house in order. Clearing can be a deeply creative and focused process that blazes a trail for fresh inspiration. Set an intention to mindfully winnow down to the possessions that fit who you are now and who you may become. As you step back and look at the things that populate your space, clarity will emerge; ideas of what you value now will bob up to the surface, as you select the clothes that suit you now and shed the ones that don't. This will help you to discover the activities that attract you now.

As I went through this process, I remember holding up my favorite business suit, which I wore when speaking at large conferences. It dawned on me that I would never again need or want to wear it. Even though I continued to speak occasionally, I wore clothes that suited me far more naturally and in which I felt utterly comfortable. I was later on a panel with Archbishop Desmond Tutu at the Dalai Lama's Conference on Seeds of Compassion. There were 80,000 people attending and thousands more watching on television. I remember thinking how my pink jacket over a black turtleneck matched His Excellency's robe.

Downsize and Disencumber

As you undertake a process of purification, you will come to know yourself in new ways. You'll feel lighter and clearer when you're done. Japanese orderliness guru Marie Kondo, author of the best-selling book, *The Life-Changing Magic of Tidying Up,* states that creating order is a spiritual task. She suggests efficient ways to prioritize the sorting of our belongings. Her method is surprisingly speedy, because instead of decluttering room by room, she advises us to tackle our worldly goods by category, starting with what is easiest to part with. So, first the clothes, then the books, then documents, then miscellany and, last and most difficult, photos and mementos. I found this to be elegantly simpler and less overwhelming than other approaches to organizing our homes. Kondo's approach includes innovative ways to fold clothing and store it on its side, which maximizes drawer and shelf space. I had to watch her videos multiple times before "getting it" and once I did, I have never gone back to "piling," where we tend to wear what's on top over and over and never get to the bottom of the pile.

Julie Morgenstern, author of *Organizing from the Inside Out*, has a marvelous term for decluttering:

SPACE – an acronym for Sort, Purge, Assign, Containerize and Equalize. I describe this in my book, *A Pace of Grace*: the Virtues of a Sustainable Life.

1. Sort: Morgenstern advises sorting in three categories: Put away, throw away, and give away.
2. Purge: Immediately take action to disperse the piles.
3. Assign: Assigning a place is identifying the ideal spot in which to place what you choose to keep.
4. Containerize: I found this to be the fun bit. Decide if you want to keep your things in a basket, a drawer or a cupboard. At first I over-bought plastic boxes for the shelves in my office, but found it chaotic to see the stuff inside. So I switched to baskets which feel gentler to me and soothe my eyes.
5. Equalize: Maintain the order you have created by following the old axiom, "A place for everything and everything in its place." I exult in the fact that I could reach into our bathroom closet blind-folded and put my hand on the bottle or jar that I want because I've learned to keep things in their places and put them back when I'm finished.

Such a simple practice of the virtue of order is deeply satisfying to one who used to treat shelves like a jumble sale and had to spend time hunting things I used every day.

Sift and Sort

As you're sorting, hold up each item and ask yourself, "Do I need this? Do I use it? Do I treasure it? Does it spark joy?" As you choose what to let go of, Kondo counsels us to thank it for its service to us, rather than merely tossing it casually on a pile. For me, this felt slightly contrived, so I adopted a general attitude of gratitude as I sorted and purged.

A good place to start is your wardrobe. For example, what you wore for business may no longer suit you. (Pun intended). I sent my business suits and "speaker dresses" to second-hand shops such as "My Sister's Closet" and "Women Mean Business." Imagining a woman walking into a job interview with confidence, wearing one of my "power" outfits, gave me a sense of righteous joy. For me this winnowing of my wardrobe clarified and confirmed that I was no longer willing to stay on the road for months at a time on speaking and media tours. I kept two of my favorite outfits and let go of the rest. I couldn't believe how spacious my previously jammed closet became. Little did I know at the time that I was going to attract a whole new mode of dressing to wear since moving to islands in the Pacific. I have a simple, beautiful wardrobe of colorful Polynesian "Aloha" print blouses I wear with capris or pencil skirts which suited me fine on our South Pacific island of Aitutaki, and now in Hawaii.

When we first moved to the Cook Islands, a seamstress stitched me up some muumuus, which were very comfortable and put me automatically into the older mama category. One day, a friend who sews and is known for her blunt honesty, said, "Linda, you're too young (she must have meant in spirit!) to wear those mama muumuus. Let me make something for you." She presented me with a hip length short sleeved blouse in a bright gold and tan flowered fabric I would never have picked for myself, and a knee-length brown pencil skirt. "You look twenty years younger," she said. I felt very comfortable wearing it, with a flower behind my ear. When I agreed to make a presentation for the Cook Islands health care agencies on virtues as tools for healing, and saw a photo of myself, I realized how right this new look was for me. I feel more myself in this new attire, and now have several blouses in bright pink and coral, deep blues, and other vibrant colors. Each blouse cost about $7 U.S. They skim over the bits I wouldn't want to emphasize and are more flattering, I admit, than the muumuu look.

Redefining Your World

Before we made the momentous decision to transplant ourselves to a small island in the South Pacific, I harbored a secret dread that Dan – scholar, Renaissance man, collector of a massive amount of books, music, electronics and tools – would die before I did, leaving me to dispose of an entire building chock full of his complex miscellany. This was the large out-building beside our home in Canada, formerly a carpenter's workshop, which Dan, my brother John and I used as our office to create The Virtues Project. Eventually, Dan took it over as his own, and expanded into it exponentially. Once our decision was made to move to the South Pacific, we miraculously cleared most of it out within three days with a garage sale, many deals and giveaways. It was like ripping the bandage off quickly. Now, my husband has his extensive and still growing library of music and books in electronic form, and even returns one book before "borrowing" another from Kindle Unlimited. His massive tastes require hardly any space at all.

Eve's Story: The Art of Disencumbering

My best friend from high school, still my sister-friend six decades later, Eve called emptying our house "disencumbering." A few years later, she and her husband did the same. They moved from a four-bedroom, 5000 square foot home in a U.S. northern suburban area to a 2500 square foot home in a 55+ planned community in the Southwest.

She says, "The house is still large by many people's standards, but we were so used to having our individual spaces and to having space for visitors that we were reluctant to change our day to day comfort level any more than that. Now that we have lived in our new home for a year, I think we would have been content with a smaller size home, as well."

"Follow your bliss and the universe will open doors where there were only walls."
Joseph Campbell, author

The Vacuum Law of Prosperity

Learn to bless and release what no longer fits your dream. Even if you have the most extensive and magnificent collection of figurines in the world, they don't travel well. If your dream is to travel, let them go to good homes. Keep a few of your favorites. That's no more than three!

From the 1930s to the 1950s, books on "prosperity thinking" became popular. During the Depression, businessman Napoleon Hill wrote *Think and Grow Rich* about the power of thought to create wealth. In 1952, Norman Vincent Peale wrote his classic, *The Power of Positive Thinking.* He said, "Formulate and stamp indelibly on your mind a mental picture of yourself as succeeding. Hold this picture tenaciously. Never permit it to fade. Your mind will seek to develop the picture...Do not build up obstacles in your imagination."

Peale advises us to expect the very best in life, imagine it and then write it down as an affirmation in present time – "I do", rather than "I will", "I am", rather than "I will be". Prosperity thinking includes a key to the attraction of wealth, whether in love, happiness, work, money, or adventure. It's called "The Vacuum Law of Prosperity."

It involves two principles which relate to clearing and cleaning:

First, we need to create a vacuum by letting go of old things, so that the new can flow in. Second, we have to give to get. Generosity magnetizes bounty.

Transcendental philosopher Ralph Waldo Emerson's famous essay of 1841, *Compensation*, highlights the basic law of prosperity that one must "give full measure for the good you wish to receive." So, as we clear out things that no longer fit us as we are now, we can pass them on as potential treasures to others, who may well receive them as things of great value.

Honestly speaking, I feel that books like "The Secret" claiming that we are in control of whatever comes into our lives, go to absurd extremes. They take a truth and over-inflate it. Are we accountable for every illness, a failing economy, an epidemic, or personal tests that come out of the blue? This theory omits destiny, mystery and Divinity.

What does resonate from that philosophy is that most of us use too little of our own power to influence our lives and respond ably as resilient thrivers, rather than reacting passively to what happens, as mere survivors. I do find that when we act with determination and trust, we do indeed attract more abundance and grace.

The act of clearing a cabinet or a life of the useless or the outmoded is a powerful invitation to the new. People afflicted by the compulsion to hoard, live under a cloud of unworthiness and emptiness. De-hoarding is a spiritual act by which we release hopeless beliefs and fears about lack, insufficiency and poverty. Holding onto unnecessary belongings clogs our space and prevents flow. They are a constant reminder that we don't have enough and we are not enough – the essence of scarcity thinking. The tide has to go out before a new tide can come in. Taking time to fashion a dream offers a fresh opportunity to have nothing in your life that you don't find useful or consider beautiful for the life you're building now.

Release Ruthlessly

After I spoke on The Virtues Project at a conference during the United Nations Year of the Family in Salt Lake City in 1994, a crowd of people rushed up and surrounded me, all talking at once and thrusting out their business cards. The founder of the Glory of Home Foundation was one of them. She grabbed my arm and pulled me into a side room. She spoke about the power of "the radiant point." She explained that you identify something you possess which fits your life and your home perfectly, whether a favorite outfit or a piece of art. Then you bring everything you own into alignment with it, releasing anything that you do not love as much or consider as essential.

One of the best ways to clear a space for a new way of life, with its daunting and delicious freedom, is to literally clear your living space of what no longer fits you at this season. From old clothes you will never wear again to books someone else may want to read, to files you will never open again, clearing away the physical debris around you has a miraculous purifying impact on your spirit. It is a powerful exercise that gives you a breath of fresh intention. It removes untouched pockets of anxiety, and unattended demands. It can actually heal long held shame.

Charles's Story: Crossing a Threshold

Charles was a Canadian university professor who had a serious problem with clutter. He rationalized the chaos in his home office, by considering the piles of papers and books "possible research", or by telling himself he just didn't have the time to deal with it at the moment. The truth was, he found it utterly overwhelming to even think of cleaning it up. Then he attended a Pace of Grace *workshop Dan and I were giving in California. He deeply enjoyed the retreat in a lodge amidst towering pines. He was amazed at the real gift he took away – a commitment to creating a space of grace.*

He later told me he had cleaned his office to the point where he could see the floor of his den for the first time in years. He said, "I crossed a threshold in my known life." Charles was exhilarated by this act of purification, which energized him, and opened the pores of his soul to new ideas as well as the freedom to move and breathe in his private space. In the process of cleaning, he cleared away overdoing, the heavy burden of procrastination, and years of accumulated guilt over what he wasn't accomplishing. As the layers of dust and detritus lifted, new energy and fresh inspiration welled up, infusing him with gratitude and quiet joy.

When we clear our space, we release guilt over all the undone projects. To be able to create a dream of positive change, we need to remove the blocks to our abundance.

"Create in me a clean heart, O God; and renew a right spirit within me."
Psalm 51:10

Reflection Exercise 5: Create a Space of Grace

- Decide to declutter a space in your home that overwhelms you. Follow decluttering expert Julie Morgenstern's SPACE concept to Sort, Purge, Assign a place, Containerize and Equalize. This is a brilliantly simple way to approach even the most daunting clearing job.

- Take a safari in your wardrobe. First identify your favorite outfits – ones that make you feel strong, attractive, and natural. Choose one that fills you with confidence, and that you expect to wear most at this season of your life. This is your radiant point. Bring everything else into alignment with how it makes you feel, whether something sporty or dressy. Follow Marie Condo's guidance: Do you love it? Does it spark joy? Bless and release the things you no longer want or need and find good homes for them.

As you clear your space, indulge in reflection about the person you want to be and the habits you want to replace. Reimagine your relationships as you wish them to be, and think on the virtues you want to cultivate. As your physical environment comes into order, your spirit will receive fresh clarity. Order banishes chaos and confusion.

CHAPTER SIX

ENTER YOUR FREEDOM SEASON

"To let go is to release the images and emotions, the grudges and fears, the clingings and disappointments of the past that bind our spirit."
Jack Kornfield, author, *A Path with Heart*

Decluttering goes far beyond tidying up our physical environment. We are even more deeply impacted by emotional and spiritual clutter – outmoded stories we tell ourselves about our limitations, judgments we hold against ourselves or others, and seeing ourselves as victims. Our identity is riddled with things that dim our natural joy, weaken the rigor of our accountability and suppress our potential to live fully and freely. When we call on the virtue of detachment, it guides us to new freedom.

Detachment has very bad press, but as a virtue it is an uplifting practice that allows us to transcend our experiences and view them from a higher viewpoint. Detachment allows us to act rather than react, to choose our responses to our own lives as they unfold.

Change the Narrative of Your Life

Whenever you embark on a path of major change, a pristine opportunity arises to change the narrative of your life. It brings a chance to take a long, loving look at the old story you've told yourself for years, perhaps all your life. Familiar examples are: "I'm never enough." "If I'm not perfect, no one will love me." "You can't trust anyone not to abandon you." "I'll never measure up." The first step in shedding self-imposed limitations is to courageously explore them. Then to name them. There is hope for us to release them only if we view them with a healing attitude of compassion.

"Life is a daring adventure, or nothing at all."

Helen Keller, American author

Take Flight

At times, one is called to make a total departure from life's current circumstances, in order to leave an impossibly stressful situation. It's a question of emotional, spiritual, and sometimes physical survival. One such circumstance is when an individual is trapped in an abusive relationship. There is more than one way to define "life-threatening". It may be the life of the soul that is at stake. Some divorces occur for that reason, and sometimes it involves divorcing one's family.

Georgia's Story: Leaving Home

Georgia, at age 20, realized that if she did not escape her mother's relentless control and abuses, with the expectation that Georgia would remain beside her in the years to come, she might never be free. Her mother had shamed her for years, mocking her for being overweight, serving her a plate of food, then taking most of it away, to "help" her lose weight. The constant haranguing left her with an eating disorder that plagued Georgia for years. There was constant hitting and beating, from early childhood through her teens, and much of that period was lost to suppressed memories.

She had been gifted with a guitar on her twelfth birthday by a relative who knew her love and talent for music. Her mother forbade her to play it, and hid it from her. Music was "self-indulgent," defying her plan that Georgia would go to university, then follow an uncle's footsteps and become a doctor. Anything hinting of fun or joy was "not God's will." Georgia became confused about religion, because of the ways it was weaponized to guilt and shame her.

For a while, she moved in with the family of a friend she had met in high school, and made them promise not to tell her mother where she was. She got a job and started saving her money. One day, her mother opened her bedroom door and stormed in. She had found out where Georgia was staying and demanded that she come home. It was then the young woman knew she had to make a more radical change.

During the hours her mother believed she was in class at college, she worked as a server. She finally saved enough money to fly to another city. There, she faced her fears of being on her own, and went through months of depression, but still had the courage to pursue her dreams of playing keyboard and composing music, which she performed in clubs. With her best friend, she flew around the world for a year, seeking adventure. She literally climbed mountains. She met people from all over the world, who loved and celebrated her for who she was. She dove deeper into her music.

When she landed again, Georgia decided to enter a healing program, to face her trauma head on. Gradually, she recreated her own narrative about herself, recognizing her beauty, and her value. She reached out to an Aunt, went to visit her, and they talked for hours. They developed a close, loving relationship, which became a new anchor for her sense of belonging. She developed close friendships with others in the world of music. Georgia was rebuilding family in a new way. She began to experience what it was like to be genuinely happy and free of guilt. For her, this required detaching from her mother, giving up an inheritance, which came with an impossible cost – one she was no longer willing to pay.

Be Adventurous

Stepping out of your ordinary life, whether by travel or welcoming a new experience, can bring a whole new perspective. I've experienced a number of life-changing opportunities in my life, one of which involved a young Tahltan medicine man in the Yukon. I had the privilege of meeting Robert at a Virtues Healing Retreat I facilitated in northern Canada, invited by an indigenous chief in the region. One afternoon, I looked into Robert's eyes, and asked him, "Who are you?" He smiled and said, "You see me." Up to then, he had not declared to anyone that he was a shaman, and for years thereafter I was one of only a few who knew and benefited from his special medicine.

Several months after we met, he invited me for a Vision Quest on the sacred ground of his people, which they had inhabited for 10,000 years. Before he left me alone in the wilderness, he conducted a prayer ceremony for me. He received a mysterious message for me while he was chanting a prayer. "Creator has a sense of humor with you, Linda. God said 'Catch the rabbit'." Shortly thereafter, Robert pulled away in his battered blue truck.

During the vision quest, I sank deep into solitude, and as Robert predicted, a grandfather eagle flew down and watched over me. A fox taught me about the power of what I came to call "contemplative vigilance" – the state of patient alertness while awaiting truth or guidance to be revealed. When foxes hunt for rabbits, they don't run around madly. They become utterly still until they catch sight of the goal – a rabbit. Then they move like the wind and pounce. For me, this meant I needed to give up my goal-driven, pressuring ways. Instead I found that resting in the guidance of "Be still and know that I am God" was to trust the process beyond my own frail efforts, to await an opportunity with patience and quiet discernment, alert to whatever comes. And when it came, to respond swiftly and decisively. Several months after my vision quest in the Yukon, I was sitting in a hotel courtyard thousands of miles away, with a business associate with whom I had just agreed to a joint project. In this highly unlikely environment, a rabbit suddenly hopped by. I smiled knowingly, taking this as a confirmation that the deal was a wise one.

"If thou wouldst hearken to my words, release thyself from the fetters of whatsoever cometh to pass. Nay rather, under all conditions thank thou thy loving Lord, and yield up thine affairs unto His Will that worketh as He pleaseth. This verily is better for thee than all else, in either world."

Selected Writings of Abdu'l-Baha, Baha'i Faith

One of the most intriguing things Robert said to me was: "Do you want to be driven or do you want to be led?" I came to understand that it was my own choice, whether to succumb to the demands of my ego – the insistent self – or free myself to follow the guidance of my soul. Being driven is a reactive way of living, which involves constant pressure, lusting after outcomes, succumbing to fear, resentment, competition, and anxiety, believing that if we just work hard enough, we will be in control. Being led is to trust life's unfolding, to cultivate our inner vision, to listen to Spirit. It is a far more peaceful, meaningful and productive way to live. It's a form of spiritual efficiency.

From Age-ing to Sage-ing: Insights about the Joys of Detachment

(With gratitude to the unknown author whose words are posted on Facebook)

"I asked one of my friends who has crossed 70 and is heading to 80 what sort of changes he is feeling in himself? He sent me the following very interesting lines, which I would like to share with you:

- *After loving my parents, my siblings, my spouse, my children, my friends, now I have started loving myself.*

- *I just realized that I am not "Atlas". The world does not rest on my shoulders.*

- *I now stopped bargaining with vegetable & fruit vendors. A few pennies more is not going to burn a hole in my pocket but it might help the poor fellow save for his daughter's school fees.*

- *I pay my waitress a big tip. The extra money might bring a smile to her face. She is toiling much harder for a living than I.*

- *I've stopped telling the elderly that they've already narrated that story many times. The story helps them walk down memory lane and relive the past.*

- *I have learned not to correct people even when I know they are wrong. The onus of making everyone perfect is not on me. Peace is more precious than perfection.*

- *I give compliments freely and generously. Compliments are a mood enhancer not only for the recipient, but also for me. And a small tip for the recipient of a compliment, never, NEVER turn it down, just say "Thank You."*

- *I walk away from people who don't value me. They might not know my worth, but I do.*

- *I am learning not to be embarrassed by my emotions. It's my emotions that make me human.*

- *I have learned that it's better to drop the ego than to break a relationship. My ego will keep me aloof whereas with relationships I will never be alone.*

- *I have learned to live each day as if it's the last. After all, it might be the last.*

- *I am doing what makes me happy. I am responsible for my happiness, and I owe it to myself. Happiness is a choice. You can be happy at any time. Just choose to be.*

I decided to send this to all my friends. Why do we have to wait to be 60 or 70 or 80? Why can't we practice this at any stage and age?"

Free Yourself from Shame and Doubt

"Remember that self-doubt is as self-centered as self inflation. Your obligation is to reach as deeply as you can and offer your unique and authentic gifts as bravely and beautifully as you're able."

Dr. Bill Plotkin, author *Soulcraft* and *Nature and the Human Soul*

My husband and Bill Plotkin are colleagues. Bill is a psychologist, wilderness guide, and author with an incredible depth of wisdom. Dan is a clinical pediatric psychologist and the wisest soul I know. Dan and I started giving workshops and retreats called "A Soul Full Life" combining virtues with Bill's description of the spiritual journey. He speaks of the blossoming of the self as a way of coming home to our true purpose and connecting deeply with nature, beauty and our own spirit.

How does personal growth actually happen? It isn't merely about resolving to give up spiritual sloth or bad habits of self-doubt. It is nearly impossible to simply stop a habit, regardless of how self-defeating we know it to be. Instead, we must *replace* it. Focusing on not doing something keeps us locked into the old idea. Replacing it by doing something new based on a new story, thereby starting a new practice, frees us to follow a path of genuine transformation.

In the years I've been researching, writing about and practicing virtues, I have experienced the simple and profound power of consciously choosing a virtue in even the most extreme circumstances, even when the ego is putting up an almighty fuss, attempting to stay in control. We can indeed change our story by choosing to live as mindfully as possible.

The story is told of a Native American grandfather talking with his grandson. "Inside all of us are two wolves, my boy. They are in a desperate fight for our souls. One is greed, fear, envy, lust, hatred, anger, and shame. The other wolf is love, trust, kindness, compassion, truthfulness, integrity, and joy."

"Grandfather, which wolf will win?" asked the boy.

Grandfather replied, "The one you feed."

Feed the Good Wolf

A small book based on ancient Toltec wisdom is *The Four Agreements* by Don Miguel Ruiz. The

Toltec Tradition comes from an ancient Mesoamerican culture, rich in teachings that encourage development of a profound connection to our inherent wisdom, power, goodness, and divinity. My personal mission is to make the sacred accessible in everyday life. So, I love short, clear steps that help us cultivate the virtues of our soul, the qualities of our character. Here is a brief description of what Ruiz wrote in his book, through the lens of The Virtues Project:

"Let your yes mean yes and your no mean no."
Mathew 5:37

Agreement 1: "Be impeccable with your word." Speak only truth. Tell yourself and others the truth at all times. Don't entertain illusions. Say only what you mean. Be completely trustworthy when making commitments. Avoid making promises you may not be able to keep. Better to reflect on a request and say "I'll think about it," than to impetuously promise something you later will regret.

Purify your words and thoughts of negativity. Avoid using your words to speak against yourself or to gossip about others. Replace negative self-talk with virtues language, even when correcting yourself. "I need to use more tact," rather than "What an idiot I was to insult that person!" According to spiritual teacher, Eckert Tolle, "Awareness is the greatest agent of change." Negative judgments of ourselves block transformation. Observing our behavior *without judgment* opens space for a new way.

Use the power of your word in the direction of truth and love. Language shapes character. It's the vehicle of thought. So, when your words are weighty, weigh your words. Speaking The Language of Virtues is the first of the Five Strategies of The Virtues Project. (See Resources)

Thinking and speaking with virtues is the most spiritually efficient cleanse we can undertake, opening us and everyone around us to our truest possibilities. Giving someone a virtues acknowledgement holds up a mirror of appreciation and allows him or her to own the feedback. "That was a thoughtful (or helpful, loving, kind, considerate) thing to do." "I appreciate your honesty." "You showed courage today speaking up to your teacher/boss/friend."

When correcting someone, including yourself, use virtues language to avoid shaming, instead naming what is called for. "How could you have said that kindly?" "Please be patient." "Please show respect and listen to what I'm saying." "What will help me to detach from the outcome?"

> *"When you are immune to the opinions and actions of others, you won't be the victim of needless suffering."*
> Don Miguel Ruiz

Agreement 2: "Don't take anything personally." Nothing others do is because of you. What others say and do is a projection of their own reality, their own story. It's all about them! Each of us lives in our own world, including projections of our insecurities and fears onto others. If we feel unlovable or have experienced early rejection, we project uncaring disinterest onto a loved one's silence. If we question our own worth, we believe others are constantly criticizing us. We are the ones who give others the power to injure us. We are the ones who carry the shame within our thoughts and imaginings. As we mature, we begin to see this sense of worthlessness as a burden of needless pain. Only then can we lay claim to our own worth.

> *"We have met the enemy, and they are us."*
> *Pogo* cartoon by Walt Kelly

Agreement 3: "Don't make assumptions."
The saying goes that when we assume, "we make an ass out of u and me". Ruiz advises us to ask questions, rather than jumping to conclusions or making assumptions about what others intend or feel, based on our own limited understanding. We need to call on the virtues of compassion and detachment in order to walk intimately with another without taking on their feelings.

This agreement reminds me of the Virtues Project Strategy of Offering Spiritual Companioning – being fully present to another without assuming anything. Whenever someone is crying, don't assume something is wrong, or that the person is feeling sad. Tears come with many different emotions, including joy. Asking "What are those tears?" helps us to avoid presumptuous question, such as, "What's wrong?" or "Why are you sad?" Be a seeker of the truth, always, and it will not only keep you from misunderstandings and useless conclusions. It will connect you with others in a more authentic way.

Likewise, never assume that others know what you want, and if they really loved you, they would know your inner desires, be able to read your mind, and of course grant your wishes. Ruiz advises us to "find the courage to ask questions and to express what you really want. Communicate with others as clearly as you can to avoid misunderstandings, sadness and drama. With just this one agreement, you can completely transform your life."

> *"In all things God loveth the highest excellence."*
> Baha'u'llah, Founder of the Baha'i Faith

Agreement 4: Always do your best.
Ruiz says that our best is going to change from moment to moment; it will be different when we are healthy than when we are sick, have plenty of time or little time. He says, "Under any circumstance, simply do your best, and you will avoid self-judgment, self-abuse and regret." To me, giving our best means balancing impeccable

integrity and unfailing tenderness towards others and ourselves.

We need to offer our best under the circumstances in which we find ourselves. This includes being scrupulously truthful about our own responsibility, while practicing compassion for ourselves.

Bill Plotkin says that each of us has a sacred wound, inflicted by a betrayal early in life, and it is the site not only of old pain but of our greatest strengths and virtues. For example, one who has known loss and lack of love, often has the most love to give and pours it into a service-oriented role.

The worst form of what Alcoholics Anonymous calls "stinking thinking" is to blame others for our own misdeeds and mistakes. AA's Twelve Steps include making a fearless moral inventory. We need to make amends, not excuses, while at the same time finding a way to forgive ourselves. When we give our best, we can relax and trust that it is enough.

Detach and Forgive

One of the most empowering ways to claim your freedom to live as you choose to live, is to summon the courage to pause, reflect and release restrictions you have habitually endured. You may identify yourself as a victim of circumstances, and "protect" yourself from intimate, trusting relationships, or you may be stuck in a stressful role, with the erroneous belief that you are responsible for everyone and everything – what I call the E-Type Personality – trying to be everything to everybody. There is both guilt and grandiosity in that illusion.

Any major life change can awaken the detachment to shift you into fresh awareness, making release possible. Sometimes it comes in a moment of startling clarity. To disentangle ourselves from all the mind clutter, we can call on the great healer – the virtue of forgiveness. We need to forgive others who have misled, hurt or disappointed us, whether a parent, child, spouse, boss, or any person of influence. Even more importantly, and harder to do, we need to forgive ourselves.

"The truth is, unless you let go, unless you forgive yourself, unless you forgive the situation, unless you realize that the situation is over, you cannot move forward."
Steve Maraboli, Motivational speaker

Let go of Regret

Another obstacle to our freedom is clinging to regret over past actions, even when – especially when – nothing can be done about it now. This is merely useless misery and needless pain.

One summer day at an annual retreat with my sister-friends, the "She-Bears," I had an epiphany. I was talking with a few of them over a cup of tea at the long table in the riverside house we rented for a week. I was saying that no matter how hard I tried, I still couldn't forgive myself for a mistake I made when my first book had garnered a six-figure advance from Penguin in New York.

Because I had recently come down with severe post-polio, I didn't have the energy to remain at the helm of The Virtues Project, which Dan, my brother John and I had founded several years before. Neither of them wanted the role either. So, when a small group of banking professionals offered to take it over, I basically handed the money to them. Within a year, it was gone. What I couldn't forgive was my seeing the money as a guilt-laden responsibility rather than a gift, which could have sustained our family and our project for years. Because of my limiting beliefs, overshadowed by a crushing sense of over-responsibility, that windfall became a source of scarcity rather than abundance.

As I sat there in tears, Pamela began to sing, "I'm gonna lay down my burden, down by the riverside." She crossed her arms over her chest and then laid them out as if releasing a long held burden. The other women gathered around and joined in. I finally let that burden go. Since then, I have recovered, money has flowed, and sustainability has rarely been an issue. The lightness I felt at releasing the guilt and shame I'd been carrying transformed into an appreciation for the intention behind my choices – my sense of responsibility. At the same time, I resolved to open myself to the gifts of life with simple gratitude.

"Without forgiveness, there's no future."

Archbishop Desmond Tutu

Have the Courage to Be Happy

During our later years, most of us have lost someone we love deeply. More and more friends have left us behind. When a beloved spouse dies, we may feel that to move on, allowing ourselves to experience joy, and maybe even a new relationship, is disloyal to their memory. We need to ask ourselves, what would they want for us? Is it just for us to remain in perpetual grief rather than cherishing the time we have left in this fleeting existence? To honor their memory is a loving act, especially if we do something to benefit others in their name. Another way to honor our love is to spread it around, to create a new garden with the remnants of the old.

George's Story: Letting Go of Survivor Guilt

Our neighbor, George, a former announcer on BBC radio, was in his nineties when his beloved wife Eunice died. For months, he wouldn't leave the house. His family encouraged him to get back into activities he loved, such as painting, but he resisted. He was invited to spend Christmas with relatives in a nearby town, but refused to go, despite every effort his children made to convince him to come out and enjoy himself.

One day, when I was visiting George, he showed me a painting he had done before Eunice died, of the bluebell wood in England where their romance had begun. When I asked what his plans were for Christmas, he told me of the family's invitation to join them, and said, "I just can't go. Eunice died here!"

I asked him what worried him about leaving the house where Eunice died, and he just shook his head. Then I asked him, "Do you feel it would be disloyal to Eunice if you left the house and enjoyed yourself?" Tears filled his eyes, and he said, "That's it exactly." Soon after that conversation, George was able to resume a pleasurable life, taking up painting again and entering pieces in the local fair. He even won a blue ribbon for First Prize.

Reflection Exercise 6: Practice Ho'o pono pono. This is an ancient Polynesian practice of reconciliation and forgiveness. It translates into English as "correction" or "to make right". Ho'o (make) pono (right). Its indigenous Hawaiian originators understood that to harbor resentment against others hurts the person who refuses to forgive.

How can you live a joyful life when you're constantly stewing about how you've been wronged? How can you ever feel free? Avoiding others rather than reconciling almost always diverts us from our earthly purpose. It clouds our life's mission to love, serve, acquire virtues and give our best to the world. There are exceptions, though. Some individuals are so toxic and rigidly resistant to reconciliation, it is better to avoid them and to practice ho'o pono pono quietly within ourselves.

Incorporating ho'o pono pono as an inner shift takes time and practice. If you are able to master it as a sustainable attitude, you can call it to mind the moment you feel yourself judging, resenting or competing with someone. You can replace those emotions with gratitude, forgiveness, and love. Although, this isn't easy, it *is* simple. It is a practice worthy of great effort.

Here is a way to use ho'o pono pono as a meditation:

Focus on someone with whom you feel conflict, resentment or anger. Or, it may be someone you have wronged. You can do this in relationship to yourself as well.

Sit comfortably and upright. Take a few cleansing breaths.

Repeat either silently or aloud several times, slowly, each of the following:

"I love you. I honestly love you. I send my love to you."

"Please forgive me. I'm so sorry. I'm truly sorry. Please forgive me."

"I forgive you. I sincerely forgive you."

"Thank you. I'm truly thankful to you."

You can use one of many on-line versions of this meditation as well.

There is a simple prayer that is often used with the dying. If the person is verbal, you can invite him or her to repeat after you:

"I love you."

"Please forgive me."

"I forgive you."

"Thank you."

"Goodbye."

CHAPTER SEVEN

BE INDEPENDENTLY WEALTHY

"Be content with what you have;
rejoice in the way things are.
When you realize there is nothing lacking,
the whole world belongs to you."
Lao Tzu, founder of Taoism

Money is one of the biggest concerns for those
undergoing a major move or a change, including
the loss of a job or retirement. Will I make or have
enough for this season? Do I have enough to last
for the rest of my life? Can I comfortably live on
my savings or retirement income? Do I need to
drastically change my lifestyle in order to survive?
For those living in poverty, this is no mere lifestyle
quandary. It's a matter of staying alive and feeding
one's children. There is much those with means
can do personally in our local communities to
rectify social inequity and influence economic
policies, especially at the local level.

For those who do have sufficient funds to live, it's
a lofty goal to be content with what is, to make the
best of your situation and find the beauty in it. This

is an emotional and spiritual quandary even more than a material one. Both contentment and courage are needed. If you cling to the known out of fear, you may never experience the sweetness of the unknown just around the bend, or the exhilaration of a leap of faith to different work, or a simpler lifestyle that may bring you unexpected relief and joy.

Stepping back for a global view, we also need to be aware that a simpler lifestyle, with less consumption, can help to sustain our fragile planet. One participant at a climate change conference in February of 2020, said, "What we need is a new understanding of what happiness is." Another spoke of a spiritual shift from an attitude of consumption to contentment – a worthy aspiration in this market-driven global culture. Reading *No One is Too Small to Make a Difference* by the young Swedish climate activist, Greta Thurnburg and *Our House is on Fire* by her family has been eye-opening for me about how short the time is before irreversible harm befalls the planet, changes that are beyond human control. It is so easy for environmental devastation to fade into the background of our awareness because it is not treated as the emergency it is by our leaders.

Independent investigation is more important than ever, followed by a shift in our own commitments, our habits and our level of contentment with simplicity.

Align with Grace

The story goes that on a glorious spring day, two shepherds were sitting on a hillside overlooking a lush pasture where their sheep were peacefully grazing, with towering mountains in the distance. One man said to his friend, "You know, all this beauty is by my command – the bright sunny sky, our happy flocks, this magnificent vista – all is according to my will."

The friend looked around uncomfortably and replied, "How can you say such a thing? Have you no humility before God?"

He answered, "On the contrary, my friend. It is because I have surrendered my will to God's that all this is by my will too."

There is a way of being that is an alignment with Grace. It has to do with trusting the currents of life, going with the flow, being in a state of flow. For people of faith, this means seeking the will of God for one's life, mindfully reflecting on a path forward that appears right and timely. For people who put an extra "o" in the word God, it is very much the same.

When it comes to material security, which is a basic human need, there is a balance between accepting what is and taking initiative to create more abundance. Many retired people discover that taking a less demanding job outside of their usual field can be deeply satisfying. Becoming a driver, a greeter, a shop assistant, a nanny, can provide just enough extra funds to keep one comfortable. People in work that injures the earth may find deeper satisfaction in moving to a more life-giving livelihood.

Less Can be More
As we get older, we become more aware that life is fleeting, and that we need to make the most of it. That doesn't necessarily involve wishing for more, although seeking new dreams, adventures and deferred hopes may call to you. Yet, for many people as they enter a new season, particularly in terms of material possessions, less is more.

Sam and Angie's Story: Cultivating Contentment
I was en route to speak at a conference in the U.S.
when I met Sam on a plane. When he learned that I
gave personal spiritual retreats, he asked if I did
them for couples. He talked almost tearfully about
his wife Angie, who felt buried under their massive
collection of possessions in a huge mansion of a
house near Seattle, Washington. She stayed in bed
most days, stricken by one mysterious ailment after
another. She felt too weak and fearful to leave the
house, and seemed to be suffocating within a
plethora of phobias.

"Do you think she would be willing to come to a
wilderness retreat?" I said, wondering where that
idea had come from.

Two months later, Sam had somehow convinced
Angie to travel north to Whitehorse, Yukon, then
drive on to Atlin, in Northern British Columbia, to
attend a retreat I had organized. The retreat was a
canoe and camping journey deep into Atlin
Provincial Park, a wilderness area where it is
possible to sail or hike for miles without seeing
another soul. A second couple joined us, and I
partnered with a wilderness guide who had a
handmade oversized canoe and plenty of camping

gear. He knew the trails and waterways like the back of his hand. I led the spiritual retreat exercises, including a ceremony renewing the couples' vows, and my friend Doug led them in fishing, climbing, repelling, and canoeing.

One morning we bounced across the white-capped waves of Atlin Lake as the wind whipped up in anticipation of an approaching storm. It was exhilarating and slightly frightening. We pulled up to an island with a clear sand beach, cooked gourmet food over a driftwood fire and camped on the shore, surrounded by the splendor of snow-capped mountains.

We sighted bears, eagles, loons, ravens and an osprey. Within days, petite Angie transformed from a reticent, timid and fragile woman to an amazon-like wonder woman, sporting a head bandanna, shorts and sturdy hiking boots. She leapt from the canoe to help pull it ashore, went tramping off to gather firewood and threw herself into the experience, body and soul. The second couple were close friends of mine who have often told me it was the most soulful, transformational experience of their lives. At the ceremony renewing their vows at the end of the trip, Sam and Angie made a commitment to free themselves from the burden of their possessions through a major downsizing, and decided instead to seek other inspiring adventures, including taking their children along. They both discovered that their freedom was of far more value to them than their accumulated wealth. And they now leave a much smaller footprint on the environment.

There are many books and articles by authors such as financial guru, Suze Orman, on making the most of retirement, the value of delaying Social Security payments as long as possible, and spending on your needs more than your wants. The key point in gaining the independence that brings you freedom, regardless of your income or your stage of life, is to cultivate contentment, to enjoy the surprising wonders of simplicity and to resist the urge that if you can make more money, you should make more money, hoping that you still have a chance at grabbing the elusive brass ring. Or believing that if you can still carry a lot of responsibility, you should. Suze Orman herself, admittedly with some trepidation, chose to give up her lucrative and fulfilling television show in her early sixties. She scaled back on her other commitments as well, and found to her delight, that she loved having more time to spend with family and friends, more time to just be. She has discovered the secret that having an abundance of non-compulsory time is one of the truest forms of wealth.

"Tell me what you want, what you really, really want."
Lyric in *Wannabe* by the Spice Girls

As you enter a new phase, you need to discern what you really, really want now. What irresistible yeses call to you? What ways of spending your precious time (and money) spark your joy? And what are the implications for your finances, if your income is changing too?

I was watching a television show on the Tiny House movement featuring an interview of one of the very first couples to adopt this minimalist lifestyle. They had one of the smallest, most space-efficient and charming homes the interviewer had ever seen, with incredibly creative adaptations for storage and multi-use items. This couple, now in their late seventies, were utterly content with the simplicity of their life. "We only wish we had built earlier."

One of the things I enjoy about that show is watching families moving from a large, multi-bedroom home to a tiny house, face the challenge of paring down their personal belongings to a fraction of what they've been living with. The host of the show draws lines around a small area or gives them containers, and all they can take with them into their new lives is what will fit into that space, since storage is at a premium. From the adults to the youngest child, hard choices must be made as to what they really value and what they are willing to sacrifice. As the family later adjusts to tiny house living, they report feeling happier, closer, and spending more time with each other than isolated on their individual gadgets. And they don't miss their stuff! They have discovered how little they actually need to be happy, and that less really does seem to be more.

If you are among those ready to part with excess in your life, consider that the less you have to take care of, the less money you need to maintain it. The shift in responsibility can feel like a huge release. And it frees up money for small pleasures and gifts.

Our friend, Aitutaki Larry, said, "For all intents and purposes, I'm independently wealthy. I have a guaranteed income for life, albeit small, and I'm careful how I live. I save money, and I live very comfortably." Several times a week, Larry goes out for breakfast at a gorgeous five star seaside resort, local paper in hand, to do the Sudoku and crossword over a latte. He lives on $45 per day including everything. He has a cleaner once a week (who charges $15 US). He often goes out with friends, works as a substitute teacher when he chooses to, and often offers free tours of the island to tourists he meets out and about. Above all, he is free from the necessity to work for a living – the fulfillment of the dream he conceived years before.

The Freedom to Give

"Wealth is not what you accumulate. It's what you give."
Cherokee wisdom

Lynne Twist is a global visionary who has raised awareness worldwide on eliminating poverty and fostering a sustainable environment. She teaches that money is energy that can help us to live freely and generously. She served as fund raiser for The Hunger Project and is author of *The Soul of Money*: Transforming Your Relationship with Money and Life, a book I heartily recommend. She quotes a Haitian saying:

"If you get a piece of cake and eat the whole thing, you will feel empty. If you get a piece of cake and share half of it, you will feel both full and fulfilled."

Lynne teaches that one of the great gifts of living by our needs rather than our addictive, market-fueled desires, is that we can share what we have with others. Even small amounts make a huge difference to people who live with very little. She said, "When you let go of trying to get more of what you don't really need, it frees up oceans of energy to make a difference with what you have."

Muhammed Yunus, founder of the Grameen Bank in Sri Lanka, conceived of the idea of giving micro loans to individuals to begin businesses in their villages. The majority of his recipients are women, who have a ninety per cent rate of repayment within the first year. Not only can they provide for their families with the revenue they create, but their status in the community improves greatly, and domestic abuses which were the norm are disappearing.

One of the essential ways of eliminating poverty is by supporting the business endeavors and banks owned by those struggling and striving for financial security and independence, such as African-Americans and other people of color. There is much those with financial privilege can do to contribute to this long-awaited step toward human equity.

"Thankfulness is conducive to bounty."
Abdu'l-Baha, Baha'i Faith

Individuals who choose to be thankful for what they have also tend to develop a taste for philanthropy.

Mick's Story: An Unexpected Philanthropist
I encountered a tourist on Aitutaki one afternoon and he readily shared his secret of wealth. Mick was an Australian "blokey bloke" with a definite swagger. He had a Dutch father and Irish mother – an interesting combo, bequeathing good story-

telling genes. He was happily staying in an economy hut only a few yards from the lagoon beach. "What more do you need?" he said. "Twenty years ago, I moved to Thailand. There are a lot of European ex-pats there too. I live in a bungalow with running water, a little kitchen, all the amenities I need, and I never cook. I collect my Australian pension which is $2000 a month. My house costs me $1000 per year – per year!" he repeats, "and my visa costs $1200 a year. I go out for just about every meal, there are lots of great places to eat and a fabulous meal costs $1.50. I can't begin to spend my pension."

"What do you do with all your money?" I asked.

After delivering a bawdy comment about easy women, to which I didn't laugh or react in any way, his eyes softened, and he said, "To tell you the truth, I give it away. If someone comes to me with a good story – their kid needs tuition, their rent is due and they don't have it, whatever – I give them what they need." This outwardly rough character is living like a king with a simple lifestyle that is deeply satisfying to him, and allows him, on his limited income, to be a benefactor. He is genuinely happy, and utterly free.

Discerning Our True Wealth

Speaking as an elder, one of the pleasures of reaching an advanced age is that one learns what matters – and what doesn't. This is a highly personal process of discernment reflecting our most authentic values. Time becomes more precious, friendship more valuable, health more important, family love worthy of great care, and meaningful service a soul craving.

For some it becomes easier – and essential – to reduce, reuse and recycle. Dan and I have both discovered the importance of an environment of beauty. As I've previously shared, Dan gave away masses of vinyl recordings, tapes and CDs when we decided to leave our home in Canada and move to the tiny island of Aitutaki. He now has a huge collection of diverse music – in the cloud – from Tibetan throat singing to Johnny Cash, Eva Cassidy to the sublime Gurumel, a blind Aboriginal singer from Australia. His music takes up no space and is easy to access.

Six years after we made the move, as I wrote in the Introduction, immigration changes forced us to leave our beloved island in the South Pacific, and we migrated to Lanai, Hawaii. We are still enjoying Polynesian culture, but in a new place.

We had to sell or give away our furniture and other belongings accumulated over six years, which was far less than we had released in our prior move from Canada to the Cook Islands. For this move, we kept only the belongings that could fit into two suitcases each. In mine, I nested woven baskets – special gifts from indigenous Pacific communities where we had taught The Virtues Project – rolled favorite paintings in a tube, and brought my collection of family and friend photos, which I like to see on the wall, not merely thumb through on my phone. We gave away nearly our entire library, and now primarily use electronic versions of books. (I realize this may sound like sacrilege to book lovers.) We brought along gifted bright flowered cushion covers and fabric placemats in Aitutaki's distinctive Polynesian applique that remind us of that island we will always cherish.

Dan has printed out large color photos of our adopted island children and sunset photos he took on the beach to adorn the walls of our new, much smaller home. These touches of beauty around us, and the music we listen to is a profound source of happiness for us.

"Wealth is not a material gain but a state of mind."

Jerry Gillies, author, *The Moneylove Manifesto*

Reflection Exercise 7: Reevaluate Your Wealth

Journal the following questions. Give yourself contemplative time to dive into them and be deeply truthful.

- If there were a fire in your home and you had twenty minutes to retrieve your belongings, what would be your three top priorities?

- Assess what you're willing to let go of, and ask yourself how often you have used each item. If it doesn't still hold the meaning it once did, gift it to someone who really needs it. Enjoy your newfound philanthropy.

- Give yourself permission to think outside the box. Brainstorm as wildly as you can. Is there something you have always wanted to do? What would it cost to try it out? Are there creative ways to earn money that would also give you joy, while allowing you to save the money you need? Is it time to consider liquidating some assets?

- If you're in your later years, are you stuck on leaving money to your children rather than spending it "selfishly"? What is your freedom worth to you? Is there something you can give them now for a particular need instead, such as a family holiday? Or money toward a mortgage?

- What would freedom from excessive financial responsibility look like in your circumstances? If simplicity is calling to you, trust that you will still be you without the earthly trappings.

- What steps are you taking, and what more can you do to help create a sustainable environment for our planet?

- What steps can you take to help alleviate poverty in your community, and give a hand up to those seeking social and economic equity? In what simple ways can you share – your time, your food, or your presence?

CHAPTER EIGHT
CREATE NEW BOUNDARIES

"We teach people how to treat us."

Dr. Phil McGraw, author, *Relationship Rescue*

At each bend in the road, each change of our circumstances, we would be wise to recalculate our personal boundaries, revising the parameters for how we choose to use our time, money, and energy. It also presents an opportunity to assess our relationship habits.

In my years speaking internationally on The Virtues Project strategies, including the third strategy of Setting Clear Boundaries, I often saw a puzzled look on the faces of listeners who had no idea the meaning of the term "boundary".

Boundaries are like the banks of a river. There are times when the boundaries need to narrow and times when we need to expand them. Boundaries are about deciding what we're willing and not willing to live with in our relationships, including the way we relate to ourselves. This involves even the way we choose to think and speak. The language we use about ourselves is a direct expression of either shame or self-esteem.

What words do you use about yourself – negative labels or affirming, encouraging words? Criticism or virtues? Virtues in the way we think and speak about ourselves and others have a significant impact on our immunity, stress levels and sense of wellbeing. Whether you call yourself "stupid" or call yourself to the virtue of wisdom makes all the difference. Calling a child "mean" versus calling her to be kind can deeply affect her self-esteem as well as her motivation to aspire to her higher nature.

Stay at Home Boundaries

There was a time during the Covid pandemic when we became accustomed to staying home more than at any time in living memory, since the rise of the Covid pandemic. Daily schedules that laid out a balance of chores, playtime, quiet time and reflection time were introduced. In order to limit exposure to the virus, many families and individuals chose to shop for groceries once a week or every two weeks, instead of dashing out spontaneously several times a week as had been their customary habit. Or they began ordering groceries online. This meant giving more attention to planning meals in order to increase efficiency in purchasing. Thousands had to allot hours each week to drive to food distribution sites in order to keep feeding their families.

An examples of how their family boundaries changed during the pandemic lockdown.

Lindi's story

Lindi, a Lecturer and Clinical Social Work Supervisor and her husband, Allan, a physician, both sixty, live in a household with their twenty-two year old son, the only one of their five children still at home, and an 18 year old friend, considered family. Allan is the only one who goes to work, as he is medical director of a hospital, thus considered essential. Lindi wrote, "Usually, we are all at work during the day, but now we are at home during lockdown. This means we are now eating meals together three times a day. I didn't want to be tied to the kitchen feeding the family all day, every day. So we had a family meeting. We agreed this was a justice issue, and that we needed a cooking and kitchen cleaning roster. We negotiated days and it worked a treat! Even Allan participated and was on the roster. We also agreed that whoever was on cooking duty was responsible for shopping for the food. This meant I genuinely didn't have to plan, prepare, or think about food on my days off.

One woman said she is using this time to move from a meat diet to a mostly vegan one, not only because of the rising costs of meat, but for health reasons. Whether aware of it or not, her shift to a plant based diet was also helping to save the planet. Also she reported that for the first time in twenty-seven years of marriage, her husband was helping in the kitchen. Amazing what boredom can give birth to!

Put New Life into Relationships

Times of change offer us a fresh opportunity to take an honest look at the vitality and happiness of our relationships, and the kindness we show and are shown by others, particularly our intimates. If we've slipped into negative patterns of "the troubled C's" – criticism, contempt, control or contention – we're free to create a new pattern of lifting each other up rather than putting each other down.

We can choose, instead, to practice the virtues of acceptance, assertiveness, and appreciation. In a thriving relationship, we accept what Vietnamese Buddhist monk Thich Nhat Han calls each other's "suchness". People don't basically change, and it is an illusion to think that anyone can control another. So acceptance of another, just as they are, is a great gift, not only to them but to ourselves. The balancing virtue is assertiveness – to speak the truth about what is just and fair, to let others know what we need, and to stop consenting to or perpetrating abusive behavior. Appreciation is the daily bread of relationships. It feeds our need to be truly seen and loved for who we are.

"If our compassion does not include ourselves, it is incomplete."

Jack Canfield, American author

Boundaries also pertain to how effectively we create sustainable practices– a pace of grace rather than overdoing or rushing, with time to be on task and time to play, rest or dream. There are bound to be times when too many projects or deadlines or games or recitals take us over the rapids, and our pace speeds up. It is at those times, we need to be mindful of returning to our natural, more graceful pace.

To regain a sense of flow, we need to ask, are we showing sufficient compassion to ourselves? How do we return to practicing life-giving balance? Are our priorities in the right order for our own wellbeing? When our own cup is full, we have far more to give others. Ideally, we choose to balance care for others and care for ourselves.

I find that I have to pause on a regular basis to do what I call, a "Discernment Map", laying out on a single page all the activities that take my time and energy, and then asking myself which ones are draining, sustaining, mere duty, or igniting joy. More on this later in this chapter. Once I see it laid out before me visually, I can make the choice to regain a new balance, spending less time working on tasks and more time playing, which for me is going to the beach with a friend, reading a good novel, or using my creativity in writing, a service project, or getting creative in the kitchen.

Even (Especially) Caregivers Need Boundaries

Far too many people who care for infirm or ill loved ones succumb to illness or even death before the ones they are caring for. According to research on aging: "Rough statistics show that thirty percent of caregivers die before those they are caring for." Some studies show deaths at a higher level. Hard as it may be to believe, 70 percent of caregivers over age 70 are said to die before the person they are caring for. It's called "Caregiver Syndrome."

In a report, *"Caring for Persons with Dementia,"* Dr. Jean Posner, a neuropsychiatrist in Baltimore, Maryland, referred to caregiver syndrome as "a debilitating condition brought on by unrelieved, constant caring for a person with a chronic illness or dementia."

According to a report from the National Consensus Development Conference on Caregiving, the most common psychological symptoms of caregiver syndrome are depression, anxiety and anger. Much of this information came from a report written by Dr. Andree Leroy, a psychiatrist in Boston.

Illness that doesn't lead to death is rampant, as well; depression and auto-immune diseases are high on the list. Caregivers often don't find time to go to their own doctor appointments. They put them off, because they're "too busy" dutifully taking care of others.

One of the red flags to be aware of is creeping compassion fatigue. It's impossible to sustain constant sacrifice of one's own health without serious consequences. Compassion fatigue can serve as a helpful sign that it's time to do some serious self-care. One of the boundaries that allowed me to sustain myself while caring for my brother for fifteen months (instead of the predicted three months' terminal diagnosis) was taking time for a daily walk and a nap. I also had the ear of my compassionate mother-in-law, who was herself a caregiver of her son, who was also terminally ill.

Practice the Magic of Moderation

In the past, as an author of several books, I was willing to review books written by others, to spend hours on the phone consulting with colleagues and mentoring individuals, as well as coping with hundreds of emails a week. Now I am no longer willing, nor do I have the mental capacity to stretch myself in these ways. I crave the freedom of spaciousness, silence, time to be in beauty, to stare at the waves on the beach, to write. I choose my interactions with care.

Elder hood is a time for being more than doing, for "sage-ing" as well as ageing. Any elder willing to share wisdom can be considered a sage. Mentoring younger ones respectfully is deeply satisfying to us and inspiring to them. (If these two effects are missing, it probably falls into the category of unwanted advice!) As we age, we no longer have the "bandwidth" to respond to others' needs as we used to. It's essential to be assertive as we clarify our personal boundaries.

I am still quite socially active, and am involved in a number of faith and volunteer activities, which nurture my soul. Yet, I continually seek a sustainable pace of grace from day to day. Setting clear boundaries is an eminently conscious decision to safeguard our own worth and happiness. It includes having the humility to accept our physical, emotional and spiritual limitations.

Honestly speaking, I lose sight of this regularly, and get caught up in things for which I have a passion, then have to gently call myself back to the reality of my actual emotional and physical capacity at this season of elder hood. It's a challenge to act my age, and it requires respectful attention to recalculating my boundaries.

Know When It's Time to Change Rules and Roles

Setting Clear Boundaries to safeguard the harmony and wellbeing of the family needs to change when our children become teenagers or even sooner. As they get older, children need to participate in working out fair boundaries around sharing family chores, curfews and other safety measures, as well as reasonable consequences for violating them. If they are included as agents of decisions about boundaries, they are far more likely to commit to keeping them.

Those of us who have adult children also need to reassess our boundaries with our children. Our adult children need to cultivate their independence. Are we going to be obstacles to that natural progression or advocates? We need to find authentic ways to support and encourage them as independent adults, not foster their dependence on us. Will we continue to pay for things that they can now afford, perhaps even more than we can? We are no longer responsible for the decisions and choices they make. That's a big attitude adjustment, yet is well worth the emotional stretch. It allows the relationship to come into a new authenticity and intimacy.

The phenomenon of "boomerang children" is increasing in the United States. Kids go off to college or to a new job, and then when they lose the job or the scholarship, they return home to "their" room, expecting Mom or Dad to continue doing their laundry and providing three squares a day.

A friend of mine, struggling to bring in income during her retirement by substitute teaching, suddenly realized that it was time to stop funding her children's travel when they came to visit her, or whenever they asked for her financial help. She needed her earnings for her own survival and to save for her own bucket list of travel. She also realized she was fostering dependency past its usefulness.

Your children are not your children.
They are the sons and daughters of Life's longing for itself.
They come through you but not from you,
And though they are with you yet they belong not to you.

You may give them your love but not your thoughts,
For they have their own thoughts.
You may house their bodies but not their souls,
For their souls dwell in the house of tomorrow,
which you cannot visit, not even in your dreams.

Kahlil Gibran, author, *The Prophet*

I'm the first person to advocate responsible parenting – particularly of children in the first six formative years, when character is actively developing. Yet, there are many other factors that impact how a child grows and develops. As soon as they go to nursery school, their peer group becomes a powerful priority. They want to act and talk like each other, dress alike, and follow the latest play fads, from marbles to electronic games. They are memorizing complex dance and song routines from online media such as Tik-Tok from the age of three. Back in the day, I remember a four-year-old boy who attended nursery school with my son, refusing to get dressed unless he could wear a shirt adorned by the Izod alligator logo!

Despite the knowledge that our children's character is shaped largely by their overall environment, some of us carry a burden of fear that we have failed as parents. The ensuing guilt brings about a false sense of responsibility for our adult children. When they are on (or over) the brink of a bad decision (i.e. one we don't approve of), we feel obligated to lecture, pressure and nag them with our presumed wisdom. Yet, in their adult years, our role as loving parents is to help them discover their own wisdom. A piece of advice can appear to them as harsh criticism. On the other hand, a perceptive question helping them to dive into their own discernment may well be received as a gift.

Know When to Speak Up and When to Shut Up

Learn to zip your lip and choose your battles. If you see your adult child making what you consider a poor decision, there are tactful ways of talking to them about it, which is the only way you have the slightest chance of being heard. Blurting out your opinion that they're being stupid will only make them (or anyone) defensive. Lecturing them automatically sets up a wall of resistance. The less you lecture or try to guilt them into something, the more likely they are to listen when you decide to share your own view. Do you want to be the force against which they rebel? The wall against which they leverage a high pole-vault maneuver?

Respecting their right and freedom to make even poor choices is the only way they will grow or learn from their mistakes. So, don't be a jewel thief. We mustn't steal away their teachable moments. This is *their* soul work, not ours. We have enough to do learning from our own teachable moments. Seeking understanding and self-discipline takes great honesty and intense effort. It takes real mental effort to summon detachment, tact, and serenity in the face of inevitable family drama.

"Time for us to step back and be forces of love."

Evelyn Eiras Belzer, a wise and beloved friend

However, respect doesn't mean saying nothing. If you decide you want to show your love and interest by saying something, first stop and think clearly what you want to say and how you want to say it. Only then, free your tongue from the vice grip of your teeth, perhaps asking a question, such as "What went into your decision to leave your wife and baby?" or even simpler, "How can I support you through this change?"

Juanita's Story: Companioning versus Control

Juanita was in shock when her daughter Maria revealed that she was considering an abortion of a surprise, unwanted pregnancy – her first. She said to her mother, "I'm really scared to have this baby." Juanita decided to offer spiritual companioning rather than to react emotionally.

133

Juanita asked, "What are you scared of?" It turned out that her daughter was afraid of losing her freedom to travel, to go wherever she wanted, and she was also the sole support for her partner. She couldn't envision how her full-time, very responsible position could mix with motherhood. Her mom helped her to get to the heart of the matter and listened patiently, with compassionate curiosity. Then she expressed her own view respectfully: "I'm concerned that in the future you'll regret aborting this baby. What do you think?"

Maria then told her of a dream she had of a child holding out his arms to her. She decided to stay the course and became quite happy about having the baby. He's a gorgeous child with a sunny disposition. The young woman hired a nanny who also does housework, freeing her up to spend quality time with her son whenever she is home. Often, Juanita is delighted to care for her adorable grandson.

I had a huge wake-up call about my role with my adult children and grandchildren. It occurred on a day of absolute chaos and multiple family dramas – all conveyed electronically from three different countries at once. It was like a hurricane, winds coming from all directions, threatening to blow me off my feet – until something strange happened. I was attempting to pray about it all, while distracted by the barrage of message pings. Suddenly a huge laugh bubbled up inside me. It was a cosmic laugh – a swift spiritual shift into detachment, humility and acceptance. I realized there was no way I could solve all these family issues. In fact, trying to do so would be interfering with others' soul work. I realized this was their journey, not mine.

Any wise words I might have had could have been easily misinterpreted as taking sides. Most importantly, it is not for me to judge the actions or decisions of my children and grandchildren, who are now responsible for their own lives and have been for some time. Compassion for their struggles can all too easily morph into codependence, with me taking responsibility for sorting them out. All this does is to encourage spiritual laziness. It's far better to respect their choices, even if I think I see a better way. So, I kept my silence, took a big step to the side (where I belong) and sent brief replies such as to one of my sons and his partner, "I know that you two can work out your relationship, and set good boundaries. I'm committed to never again participating in a conversation that crosses the line of your privacy." Whew! I narrowly avoided getting in over my head, allowing those emotional winds to catch me up and bring me right into the fray, as judge, jury, and arbitrator. That's not a role I signed on for when I gave birth.

Remember that our influence over our children is at its zenith in the first six years of life. This is the critical period for bringing out the best in them, by acknowledging and calling for their virtues of love, peacefulness, helpfulness, courtesy and respect. After that, our influence plummets alarmingly. And after age twenty-one, fageddaboudit! We have to give up being the sage on the stage and become the guide on the side. It is not our parental responsibility to prevent a divorce or rescue them from poor financial decisions. We only get to choose how we interact with them or their partners, and to find the balance between generosity and wisdom when it comes to giving them money. Caring may be sharing, but there's a limit.

Set Boundaries, Not Barriers

One elderly Cook Islands friend with limited income told family members, "You're welcome to come and visit. I'd love to see you. But I won't cook for you. You need to take care of your own food." What excellent clarity. If you have a large family, a two week visit can cost a small fortune. Everyone needs to pitch in to do the work and handle the costs of all that hospitality.

"There are only two lasting bequests we can give our children.

One is roots and the other is wings".

Johann Wolfgang von Goethe, German author

Isn't it kinder and genuinely more loving to expect our children and grandchildren to claim their independence, take responsibility for their own decisions, their own lives? To stand on their own holy ground? Don't keep them tethered to your opinions, or they will never fly. I'm learning the skills of "tongue in groove" and the KISS principle (Keep it Simple Sweetheart). When we do choose to express our opinion clearly, it doesn't bear repeating, i.e. nagging. Our children may occasionally crash, but that's how we all learn. So when they have flown on to make their own lives, let's not clip their wings with criticism or excessive advice. You have already given them roots. Help them to grow their wings.

Freeing ourselves and our adult children from enmeshment requires the deliberate practice of detachment. Detachment is a little understood virtue, since the popular use of the word means "uncaring" or "indifferent." As a quality of character and a spiritual practice, it means stepping back to gain perspective before we act, letting go of attachments and thus gaining great freedom of choice. Detaching with love is absolutely essential for sustainable, healthy relationships.

Fiona's Story: Cookies in Jail

Fiona, a woman who served as principal of an award-winning virtues school, shared with me her success with companioning her adult son. She was determined to set boundaries for herself based on compassion and detachment. He'd been selling marijuana which he grew illegally in a field hidden on his rented property, despite her warnings that one day he would get caught and needed to make something more of his life. Until she began practicing detachment, talking with him triggered her own guilt, anger, disappointment, judgments, and self-recriminations.

One day they were driving together and her son pulled over and parked. He turned to her and said,

"Mom, I need to talk to you. It's finally happened. The police discovered my operation, and I need to let you know I'm going to prison. The hearing is next week."

Fiona took a deep breath and silently called on her virtue of detachment. "I'm listening," she said, simply. He poured out the story of how the bust had occurred and talked for quite a while. She just listened with receptive silence, nodding occasionally. He paused, as if steeling himself for hand-wringing and recriminations, or at least an "I told you so."

She just smiled at him and said, "Don't worry, dear. I'll send you cookies in jail."

He told her, "Mom, this is the best talk we've ever had!" Of course. She had hardly said a word.

"Peace is not an absence of activity, but a very vibrant, vital quality of serenity where everything is in harmonious relationship."

New Thought Dictionary

Reflection Exercise 8: Boundary Setting

- Reflect on how well you're setting boundaries around your time and energy. Do they sustain your sense of balance? Do the priorities for how you use your time include activities that bring you joy and support your health? Do you include "me days" in your schedule? If not, set some up on your calendar. Identify one day or a portion of a day each week when you get to pursue whatever you want to do. Lunch with a friend, a trip to a pool, a walk in the forest, a day in bed with a good book, time to work on a puzzle or craft, or simply a day to drift and putter.

- If you have "booked" time for yourself on any given day, there is no need to explain it to anyone. You need only say, "I have something scheduled that day. Let's find another date."

- Shift into sacred curiosity – listen with detachment and compassion – rather than giving advice to someone whose choices disturb you, particularly an intimate such as a spouse or an adult child. Learn to pause before responding. See how companioning rather than attempting to control transforms the relationship. (See Resources for more on the Companioning Process). Most people simply need a listening ear of empathy, not someone to fix them.

- Make mindful agreements on your own terms, such as conditions for accepting a new job. If you are only willing to work part time, whether as a volunteer or a paid employee, make that crystal clear in the beginning and stick to your own agreement. If your employer keeps pushing for more, you can become a free-lancer, a free agent. You alone can defend your own essential boundaries; there is no one else to do it.

- Create a Discernment Map. Clockwise on a sheet of paper or a page in your journal, lay out the various activities on which you spend your time and energy. On a separate page write these four questions to apply to each thing you've listed and create a simple symbol for each one. As an example, here are the symbols I use:

Does it drain me? (tear drop)

Is it merely a duty? (box)

Does it sustain me? (cloud)

Does it ignite my joy? (sun rays)

Now, go back to your page and put these symbols beside or around each item to which they apply. This will give you a clearer picture of what in your life drains you and sustains you, and you have the choice to change the picture and adjust the narrative. This is an opportunity to set new boundaries that will nurture you and make you more effective at the tasks you choose to undertake. Ideally, you will play more and work less.

For many of us hyper-responsible folks, it can be quite a stretch to learn how to play, when one's very identity involves selfless sacrifice. These are admirable virtues, but moderation and joy are virtues too. They allow us to give far more amply and without exacting the price of guilt from those we serve.

CHAPTER NINE

PLAY IS THE NEW WORK

"This is the real secret of life – to be completely engaged with what you are doing in the here and now. And instead of calling it work, realize it's play."

Alan Watts, British Writer

When you have time to recreate and restore yourself, how do you spend that precious time? What do you do other than stare at a screen? For stay at home parents, how do you play with your children in ways that take the tedium out of being at home with them all the time? Parents who tap into their creativity invent innovative ways to play, such as setting up "zip lines" in the back yard, homemade water slides, and new family dances on Tik Tok.

Recreation is the act of re-creating ourselves. It is essential to our souls. Individuals who love and are invigorated by their work are blessed to find work and play nearly interchangeable.

Release the Bonds of Guilt

For people who are retiring, moving from the structured world of work to a more spacious life can be deeply challenging, even guilt-inducing. One of the biggest challenges is adjusting to the opportunity to indulge in true leisure.

After touring Australia, giving virtues presentations across the country, Dan and I took a "pause for applause" on beautiful Lord Howe Island. With its steep mountains and sweeping beaches, it's one of the most beautiful places on earth. A man passed us as we were coming down a sand dune and he was leaping upwards. I caught a glimpse of a phrase on his T-Shirt and asked him to stop. He willingly turned around. It said, "I just realized. I don't care." A laugh gurgled up from deep inside me.

I later had custom T-shirts made for my She-Bear women's circle, and at our next summer retreat talked to Cheryll (to whom this book is dedicated) about why this phrase touched me so. Wisely, she said, "For someone who's carried so much responsibility all her life, it means freedom." Many of us, as we age, realize suddenly or gradually that things that mattered to us before no longer have any power over us – the need to get it all done, other people's opinions and judgments, the pressure to keep plugging away, the constant demand to help anyone with needs. We give up the theme song of, "Your needs are my skills." Suddenly life rushes in like a wave leaving the sand naked with possibilities. Hey, this is my life! I need to break out of self-imposed compulsions fueled by my sense of "not-enoughness," or people pleasing, or excessive altruism, and exult, enjoy, sing a new song, and learn to be free.

Embracing freedom isn't a license to selfishness. It is simply opening to new horizons, with more agility in choosing our yeses, and a more mindful, active pursuit of joy.

Stretch Your Resilience

When life's currents carry us into a time of change, whether it involves a shattering sorrow, reorienting our compass with a move, leaving a long time job with which we deeply identify, or readjusting to a new normal because of illness, a fresh opportunity arises to change our minds, our plans, and our ways of living.

I've witnessed marvelous examples of resilience in people I've had the privilege to companion in their last days of life on earth. Even in their final hours, some souls choose to focus on pleasant things and simple joys. They seem already to be resting in peace.

Mary's Story: Savoring Beauty at the End of Life

On my first Hospice spiritual care visit to Mary, while she was still able to function at home, she was sitting on the couch, plugged into an oxygen tank. She was a lovely, silver-haired woman of sixty-three, with a diagnosis of terminal emphysema. After introducing ourselves, the first thing she said to me, with a wistful smile was, "I'm just haunted by these words: 'Her ways are ways of pleasantness and all her paths are peace.' I simply cannot remember where I read them."

I looked it up and discovered it was from Proverbs 3:17, speaking of the virtue of wisdom. "She is more precious than rubies: and all the things thou canst desire are not to be compared unto her." I continued to visit with Mary after she was admitted to hospice as an in-patient. As her physical condition deteriorated, what struck me was that she still seemed content and happy, dwelling in a rich inner world. One day when she could hardly speak for breathlessness, she whispered to me, "People feel sorry for old people. But they don't understand. They don't know...There are things...beautiful things." Her eyes were luminous

"What things, Mary?"

"Words. The beauty of words."

One day it occurred to me to ask her if she had ever done any writing. She blushed shyly and admitted she had. I asked to see something she had written, and her son brought in an old brown envelope full of short stories in faded type. I particularly remember one about a young soldier who came to tea. I could visualize the translucency of the cup he held and the slight tremor of his hand.

I was blessed to be with Mary the day she died. The nurses said she wasn't recognizing her family members and that she was in a strange state of agitation. When her relatives took a break, I slipped into the room and found her alone. She was making a high keening sound, which I matched. As our duet continued, her eyes fastened on mine and I said softly, "Words, Mary, the beauty of words. 'Her ways are ways of pleasantness and all her paths are peace.'" She gave me a radiant smile, and soon after, she went.

The Happiness Curve

The strength of our resilience depends on another virtue – confidence. We need to trust ourselves to adapt to change, as daunting as it may be. For elders, it may be helpful to know that as we age, we not only adapt to the changes in our health and energy; we tend to be happier. Polls of people at different ages in 149 countries reveal a startling pattern. When asked to rate their life satisfaction on a scale of one to ten, most adults in their early twenties reported fairly high happiness levels, with a gradual fall-off as they approached midlife. Adults reported being *least* happy in middle age, roughly between the ages of 39 and 57, with the happiness low point at age 50.

Here's the most surprising part. As they aged, older adults rated their life satisfaction much higher, with happiness ratings rising gradually and steadily from age 50 through the decade of the 90s. Researchers are calling this process the "U-curve" of happiness. When put on a graph, the results actually form a lop-sided smile. There are a number of interpretations of this phenomenon. It's not that old age is devoid of troubles, aches, pains and limitations. It's that elders tend to appreciate the ordinary, and drain every drop of pleasure from each day of life. And they take more time to play, whether in learning to play an instrument, studying a subject that interests them, or tending the garden.

Child's Play as Mindfulness

Playing with children is like entering a new world, one that is deeply focused on the senses, and sometimes wildly free. To play with a child requires fully concentrated presence and can lead to moments of wonder. To be in this state of acute awareness, one must detach from busyness and even thought, and simply be in the moment. It's almost a form of meditation. Have you noticed how often kids ask for this kind of presence? "Watch this, Daddy!" They want us to see and be with them in whatever they are doing. Going for a walk with a young child can be a sweet adventure. As they notice what is around them, follow their lead. This is best done in a place of nature, if only a backyard, but can be done anywhere, including the living room rug.

Marie's Story: Learning to Companion Children

I was giving a mandated Virtues Project parenting class in Yukon, Canada to young First Nations mothers who had been abusing their children. One had been locking her two and five year old children in the closet when she came home from work because she couldn't cope with their noise and was afraid she would hit them. In the class, she learned the life-skills of speaking virtues language, setting clear boundaries, and spiritual companioning. One way we explored the practice of companioning was for her to put off cooking dinner first thing, putting out a little bowl of nuts or fruit and just getting on the floor. I told her and the other moms, "Your kids will show you what to do to companion them." When you get on the floor with babies and young children, they climb onto you, cuddle, roll around, and laugh. The next step was to ask her older child a question, "What was day-care like today?" then to share something about her day.

On the second day of the workshop, Marie was bright-eyed and bursting to share. "I did that thing you taught us," (spiritual companioning). "I can't say it but I call it 'walk along'". My kids and I had so much fun, and we talked!" Marie learned to set a boundary for herself to spend the first fifteen minutes after arriving home on the floor or the couch with her children, giving them her full attention. Then her boundary with them was that either they helped prepare dinner or played quietly with a puzzle or book while she made dinner alone. There was no further abuse.

Fifteen years later, I met Marie on a return trip to the Yukon, when I was completing research for my novel, A Scent of Sage. *She was a waitress at a café and came over to me, saying, "Is that you, Linda?" We embraced, and she excitedly told me that she and her children still pull out* The Family Virtues Guide *to solve problems together or just name a virtue they see in each other. "It changed our lives," she said.*

Find a New Balance

"Whatever lifts the corners of your mouth, trust that."

Jalal'u'Din Rumi, Persian Sufi poet

Men and women with highly purposeful lives, including caregivers, find that it isn't easy to refocus the laser attention we've trained so long on the work to which we have devoted ourselves. Shifting attention from taking care of a high-needs loved one to ourselves often takes deep inner work. Many women have been conditioned to believe that relaxing, seeking enjoyment, or focusing on our own needs is lazy, selfish, indulgent, and not womanly at all. Men have been told that to be anything but productive to the max is unmanly. It takes courage and determination to give ourselves permission for pleasure and joy. It's not that we are now going to care any less about others. Rather we are just choosing to be more selective about what we say yes to. We're also more willing to turn the light of our awareness inward. What is play to us? How can we create a new balance that gives us an equal experience of purposefulness and pleasure, work and play?

Olivia's Story: Exquisite Balance

I met 81 year old Olivia, a volunteer with a local community organization, and was amazed at her glam factor. She's slim and fit, walks four miles a day, and has startling blue eyes and a shock of platinum hair with a layer of purple dye in the back – one of the latest trends in hair styles, which she has been doing for years. As we chatted, it was as if we were old friends, sharing easily. We had lunch together and "talked story," as we say in Hawaii.

Twenty-eight years into a wonderful second marriage, she and her husband were at home watching a movie. Suddenly, in the middle of a huge laugh, he died. The film was a comedy entitled "Love and Death!" Olivia's perspective now is that his was a good death, with no pain at all. She decided to move to her parents' then empty home in Hawaii, and has lived there happily ever since. Olivia said, "During my first marriage, I thought I would spend my life in a hammock reading a book," but when her first child started school and she was contemplating a divorce, she started work as a caseworker at a Social Services agency. "There was never a day I didn't love my job," she said.

After thirty years, she retired as director, and her colleagues celebrated her as the "first lady". She had repeatedly risen in the agency and was the first to take on each new level of responsibility as new departments required a manager. She is a collector of rare art, involving cityscapes and engineering feats and is leaving it to a grateful University of Hawaii. She often goes to concerts and art exhibitions, travels to exotic and beautiful places, her latest on a river cruise through Eastern Europe. One of her biggest challenges is juggling the men in her life, who are younger of course, and continually pursuing her.

She shared one of the boundaries in her love life. She tells a new man right off the bat that she will never marry again and that she will never live with anyone again. She prizes her solitude and her freedom. Olivia is one of the most glamorous, interesting, and relaxed women I've ever known. She took me to a European restaurant strangely situated in an industrial area in Maui, Hawaii, where we dined on delicious schnitzel and strudel. She savored every bite, as did I. To me, she is an example of someone with an ideal balance between service and pleasure, altruism and self-care. She is a maven of how to play.

Unleash your creativity

"The creation of something new is not accomplished by the intellect but by the play instinct acting from inner necessity."

Carl Jung, Swiss psychiatrist

Play doesn't mean sitting around doing nothing meaningful. It's choosing to engage in what sparks our joy, whether keeping a spotless home, or a messy studio where messy ideas breed fabulous new paintings, designs or words.

Some of us more serious folks need to consciously learn to play. Learning to play has less to do with leisure and more to do with joy. Some of us would be utterly lost without being involved in some purposeful service or engaging work, whether as a volunteer, employee, artist, or entrepreneur. Also, many retired people can use the income from a part-time position. However, in our "Freedom Season", we need to work at applying that need to something that lights us up. It can be helpful to dip our toes into a number of roles as we explore what engages us heart and soul, and what will bring pleasure rather than pressure. The world needs people who are fun to be around, cheerful and happy. To me, courting joy is a sacred obligation.

I belong to a Writers' Circle. Some members of the group have never published before and get a gleam in their eye talking about a long cherished idea of a children's book, a book of poetry or a novel. There are many ways to publish these days, including at no cost on Amazon. I'm happy to mentor them to do that, and meanwhile I'm getting excellent, discerning feedback about this, my latest book.

Another friend has had a lifelong appreciation of art, and is now trying her own hand at it, having joined a class. Her latest creation is contemplative photography which she learned during a weekend retreat. I found her first attempts exquisite – a close-up of intricate patterns on a stone, an arrangement of leaves on a forest floor, the play of light through trees.

Living on a small island means that there are many needed services, and jobs are plentiful. A friend who just turned seventy, retired from a public service job, keeps getting job offers. She immediately turns them down, since she wants nothing to do with pressured daily work. Yet, she happily spends hours on her latest creation – making banners of triangular flags out of aloha shirts she buys at the local thrift store. They have been displayed at a number of community events, adding a festive note. She also volunteers for "Meals on Wheels" and special events such as serving Christmas dinner to seniors.

Invest in Comfort

In my considered opinion, comfort is also part of the gestalt of a playful, happy life. I have a line from a magazine shoe ad in my current Vision Board that says, "If you're comfortable, you're unstoppable." With the physical changes that come with aging, I decided to invest in one luxuriantly, adjustable, comfortable recliner. I aspire to what a friend has, which is an adjustable bed. If you need to raise the head or the part below your knees, it will accommodate. Comfort gives us the needed equilibrium to live it up at times of activity.

Entertain Wonder

Get out of your self-imposed shroud, garbed in sweatpants, passively watching TV or your phone. Get out of the house. Go to the pool, take a manageable hike, plan a day of adventure with a friend, or go out to lunch in a new place. If you live in a rural area, drive to a dark spot where you can see the night sky, and do some star-gazing. The beauty of nature has more power to lift our souls than anything else in the world.

Some of the highest rated cities for lifestyle, such as Santa Fe, Seattle, San Francisco, Vancouver and Victoria, Canada, Wellington, New Zealand, Copenhagen, Denmark, Vienna, Austria and Osaka, Japan have plenty of green space, natural beauty, and access to outdoor leisure. The need to bask in natural beauty is a portal to play that uplifts and enriches.

Design Your Time

One of the ways to create a happier balance between your task list and your play time, is to plan each day and each week, with the intent of spaciousness. Block out free times in which you can do whatever you want. Plan adventures in advance and make them a priority. If your children ask you to come and mind the grandchildren for a day and you have planned either a day in bed with a good book, or a ride with a friend to a place of beauty, there is no need to justify or explain. Simply say, "Oh, I'm booked that day, dear. I'll be happy to come another time."

When energy is at a premium, pace yourself so that you have enough rest between tasks – in your comfortable chair. Read wonderful books either on an e-reader which blesses us with whatever size print we need, an audio book, or a regular book to hold in your hands. Enter other worlds through the plethora of delicious books that are available at no cost through your local library or low-cost on Amazon Prime.

"Do you know what you are? You are a manuscript of a Divine letter. You are a mirror reflecting a noble face. This universe is not outside

of you. Look inside yourself. Everything that you want, you are already that."

Jalal'u'din Rumi

Mary and Dwayne's Story: Redefining Success

I met Mary and Dwayne, both chefs in their thirties, shortly after moving to Lanai, Hawaii. They had devised a plan to allow one of them to work and support the other to play, then they would reverse roles. Mary explained, "We decided to reverse our commitment to career and focus on our values." What they valued was easy access to natural beauty, time to ski, time for leisure. Mary became immersed in learning to work with clay, and before they left Hawaii to return to their home state of Oregon, she presented me with two lovely glazed cups she had crafted at the local arts center.

I met another couple on a different island – Aitutaki, Cook Islands, where Dan and I lived for six years. They had both had high-paying corporate jobs and had made the radical choice to say yes to adventure rather than further accumulation or career advancement. Now in their forties, they had decided to travel the world. They sailed wherever the wind of their will of the moment took them. They were joyously peaceful and relaxed.

Reflection Exercise 9: Learn to Play

- How often do you give yourself a "Me-day", a mental health day off, a non-compulsory day where you have no plans and no destination but can do whatever you want? What do you need to detach from in order to claim this freedom? If you have young children, a day for yourself will refill your reserves of patience and enthusiasm for your time with them.

- Mary Pipher in her wonderful book, *Women Rowing North*, quotes Iris Murdoch: "One of the secrets of a happy life is continuous small treats." Describe three small treats that would make your day.

- How do you play? Does it involve a solitary activity or time with a friend or loved one? Brainstorm with a trusted person ways to play that are deeply satisfying to you. Then do the same for that person. Don't look down on simple, meditative activities like doing jigsaw puzzles, which can soothe the soul and detach us from thought.

- Spend some time playing with children. Look, smile, listen, touch, respond and follow their lead. It will open you to fresh imaginings.

- Choose four days in the next month as Me Days and mark them on your calendar. Just do it!

CHAPTER TEN

CULTIVATE YOUR SPIRITUALITY

"We are not human beings having a spiritual experience. We are spiritual beings having a human experience."

Pierre Teilhard de Chardin, French philosopher, Jesuit priest

Any major shift in life brings an opportunity to reinvent ourselves, to change the design of our lives. It calls us to choose mindfully, prizing this new season. We need to ask ourselves what practices we want to set our sights on. For some, it may have to do with reshaping ourselves physically – losing that weight we've meant to get rid of for ages. For others, it's a chance to replace habits we recognize as draining or deadening with life-giving ones.

In my view, one of the most transformative changes comes with focusing on our spiritual needs. Having a regular practice of reflection allows us not only to reflect deeply on our dreams at a time of change, but also to explore our spirituality.

How do you nurture your spirit and your joy? It goes beyond finding a Faith congregation in which you feel at home. It's in your daily attitudes and practices that deeper spirituality can take root.

A Working Definition of Spirituality

I use a "3M" definition of spirituality: Meaning, Mastery and Mystery.

MEANING

"Everything can be taken from a man but one thing: the last of the human freedoms—to choose one's attitude in any given set of circumstances, to choose one's own way."

Viktor E. Frankl , author, *Man's Search for Meaning*

Sadly, forty per cent of Americans report that they have no sense of meaning. Reflecting on what is meaningful to us is to explore our inner landscape, which leads to genuine intimacy with ourselves.

163

It's a search for our authentic identity. Who am I, really? What is my life about? What is meaningful to me? What do I truly value? What is my purpose – my calling – at this season?

Janice's Story: Meaning in Sacrifice

As a spiritual care and bereavement counselor at a Hospice I have companioned caregivers as they contemplate what life will be like after the loved one they've been caring for has passed on. Janice, who was her brother's primary caregiver, shared her grief with me a few days before he died. She and her long-suffering husband sold their beautiful home in a distant town in order to move where her brother wanted to be. "I'm really exhausted," she said. "I haven't slept well in years." She had been tending to her brother for three years by then. As tired as she was, she believed that it was a calling from God to care for him and was deeply glad she could do this for him. Thankfully, her husband felt as she did that this was their personal mission.

After saying she wasn't one to memorize scripture, she quoted several Bible passages to me. Her faith was at the heart of her sense of meaning and purpose. Knowing her brother's death was eminent, I talked to her about having an "LFT" –

a "looking forward to" – after his passing, something I wrote about in my book, Graceful Endings *: Navigating the Journey of Loss and Grief. I asked her what she likes to do or where she might want to go with her husband. "We need to reconnect, just the two of us," she said. "I'm not really a beach person. I love mountains and forests." She also spoke of having so many things she wanted to pursue, including painting with water colors. Every time she mentioned it, her otherwise sad face lit up with delight. I later spoke to her husband about her idea of LFT and he said he had just the right spot in mind – a lakeside cabin surrounded by forest and mountains, close enough to a city to have fun things to do there. I said, "Make sure she brings along some water color art supplies!" Just talking about her sense of purpose in serving her brother and things in which she finds joy lifted her spirits that day.*

Duty to the point of sacrifice isn't the only aspect of meaning we need to tap into. Activities that uplift our spirits, such as the arts, bring deep joy, and help to balance the meaning that comes with responsibility. Whatever magnetizes our sense of who we are is part of our spiritual development.

Victor Frankl, quoted above, is one of my heroes. He was an Austrian psychologist who was imprisoned in Auschwitz and several other Nazi concentration camps during World War II. In his life-changing book, *Man's Search for Meaning*, he described how he survived the horrors of the camps by holding to the meaning he found, even in suffering. He wrote, "Between stimulus and response there is a space. In that space is our power to choose our response. In our response lies our growth and our freedom."

Frankl developed a theory and a new form of psychotherapy based on his experiences in the death camps. He observed three sources of meaning that increased people's chances of survival far more than those who had lost all hope: first, people who had hopes of being reunited with loved ones; individuals who had projects they felt a need to complete; and people with great faith. Hope and faith are powerful antidotes, even when we have absolutely no control over the causes of our suffering.

I experienced this in my fifties in a far less dramatic way when my career as a speaker and teacher, traveling with my husband throughout the world, was interrupted by a severe bout of Post-

Polio, a syndrome that strikes people who had polio as children. It involved a recurrence of the symptoms that I had at age eleven, when I contracted Bulbar Polio, but without the presence of the virus. With Post-Polio Syndrome, the neurons and muscles doing double duty all the years since the initial episode finally tire and weaken. I was deeply fatigued, had mild paralysis, joint pain, trouble swallowing, and mobility challenges. I could only walk with a cane.

At first I could do nothing about it except surrender to acceptance. Then, one day when I was so ill, I thought I was going to die, I crept out to the living room to attempt to pray, although my brain was so fogged that I could barely put words together, much less dive into my previous practice of meditation. It was as if the screen of my mind had gone dark. Suddenly I heard a strong inner voice say, "I will give you 10 rules for health. Write them down and follow them." I quickly opened my journal and wrote what was flowing into my mind. It was as if I were taking rapid dictation. These are the 10 Rules for Health I was given:

1. Purity and Cleanliness: Outside, bathe daily. Inside, eat pure water-based foods. Eight

glasses of water a day. Dark greens, legumes, rice, root vegetables. A little meat. Cut oils by two thirds.

2. Pranha (Breathe): Learn Yoga. Walk or exercise every day for ten minutes, then fifteen, then twenty. No more. Breathe fresh air every day. You haven't breathed deeply in years.

3. Proper Vitamins: Increase B, C and E. Speak to a homeopath and listen to what she says.

4. Proactive Rest: Take two rests each day. Do it as a routine. Stop *before* you get tired.

5. Pace Yourself: You have four hours a day for work, sometimes six. Choose carefully. Keep your correspondence current. Enjoy! Enjoy!

6. Pray Every Hour: Let your movements be a prayer, your work, your daily food.

7. Pursue Peaceful Activity: Cut television down. It depresses you. Read what comes to

you. Listen to music. Clear and clean in small ways, watch the fire, write letters.

8. Play! Spend time in ways that give you joy and make you laugh.

9. Prioritize: Put your first passion first. It is your most productive activity.

10. Plan a Sustainable Life.

These rules were given to me based on my physiological needs with severe Post-Polio Syndrome. People suffering from other energy diseases such as Hypoglycemia or Chronic Fatigue Syndrome have told me these rules are the first "remedy" to really work for them. I recommend that people modify them as they and their doctor see fit while capturing the spirit and the rhythm of these principles and adapting them to their own lives.

Learning this new health-giving lifestyle restored me to the point where Dan and I could resume our work and travel for The Virtues Project. Even more importantly, I received invaluable life lessons from having to relinquish my fierce determination to overdo, and focus more on being than doing. It actually deepened my sense of meaning and purpose. I later elaborated on the 10 Rules for Health in my book, *A Pace of Grace*: *Virtues for a Sustainable Life*. The four elements of the book are: Purify Your Life, Pace Yourself, Practice the Presence, and Plan a Sustainable Life. Sometimes meaning becomes concentrated in the practice of acceptance – acceptance of things we cannot control but to which we can choose to respond ably.

"But the fruit of the Spirit is love, joy, peace, patience, kindness, goodness, faithfulness, gentleness, self-control."

Galatians 5:22

MASTERY

Another aspect of spirituality is the personal mastery that comes of consciously cultivating our virtues – stretching our capacity to trust, to experience gratitude, to love deeply, to call on discernment, to see with eyes of justice, to honor the truth, and to pursue excellence in our personal lives. These virtues are the true fruitage of our lives.

Heightening our awareness of the freedom we have to choose our responses to life –whatever our situation – leads to growing our virtues. Much of our inner work is recognizing the teachable moments that often come in the form of tests. Focusing on the growth virtues we need to develop is far more useful than wallowing in fear, shame, grief or guilt. Seeing ourselves not as victims of circumstance but athletes facing life's challenges with rigor and gentle determination changes everything.

"There is no place so AWAKE and ALIVE as the edge of becoming."

Sue Monk Kidd, author

Become a Deep Soul Diver

Whether or not we have ever ventured out of the shallows, it is never too late to dive deeper. Life is always waiting to take us to new depths of understanding and growth.

Jason's Story: His Shining Hour

Jason, a man of seventy-five, who worked as a lawyer, had a lifelong dream to be a singer. With the encouragement of friends who were successful performers, he decided to put on a one-man musical show in a high profile club for the first time. Having sung for years in his faith choir, his voice was richer than ever, and he was confident he could pull it off. Then disaster struck. When his musical director, Thomas, suddenly quit without explanation, Jason lay in bed for days, paralyzed by anxiety, struggling with panic and insomnia. Thomas had the scores for the songs, the studio for rehearsals, and had been Jason's accompanist. The show was only a couple of months away. What would he do now? Jason had been fearful all along that this was too good to be true, that he wasn't deserving of such joy. This catastrophe only confirmed it.

After talking with me and others, he pulled himself together, prayed for help, focusing on his "A-Team" of musical ancestors, angels and advisors in the spiritual realm, and did his best to replace fear with faith. He reached out to another singer, asking if she knew anyone who could serve as a musical director. Fifteen minutes later – miracle of miracles – she sent him the name of the musician he had wanted as musical director in the first place! The man was now free to work with Jason, and offered to do everything the former accompanist had done. And his studio was only a few miles from Jason's apartment. Jason was jubilant! He called me to celebrate.

"All that anxiety for nothing!" he chided himself.

After inviting him to share what the anxiety was about, I said, "You can let go of that needless pain, you know."

"No way. I'm 75 years old! My personality isn't going to change now," he said.

"Not true. You're in your freedom season. You're perfectly capable of doing your inner work. Do some deep soul diving! You can trace the roots of this pain you carry and let it go."

"Really?" he said, sounding stunned.

"Yes. There is no need for you to suffer like this anymore. It's very old stuff."

We talked about how the anxiety was bonded to his sense that he is unworthy, and that he has to do everything himself. I pointed out times when he had the courage to trust, and everything fell into place with perfect, Divine timing.

"All you need to do is discern your part and God's part, and stop trying to do God's part."

As we said goodbye, Jason sounded remarkably calm and optimistic. He later told me that on the night of the show, as he stood behind the curtain waiting to go on stage, he felt "calm and happy and bright" – the very lyrics of his opening song "My Shining Hour." The high-end venue was packed, with standing room only. He sang to two hundred of his colleagues and friends, who reacted with astonishment and exuberant applause.

The Optimist and the Pessimist

Deep engagement in spiritual exploration requires us to let go of our illusions of control and seek the flow, look for what is possible without pressure or angst, with an attitude of deep trust. Then, when we discover our own part to play, acting on it quickly and giving it our best. An attitude of openness to what is possible is critical.

There is a story about a pair of six-year-old twins – one, a total pessimist and the other, a complete optimist. Worried about their extreme personalities, their parents brought them to a counselor. To brighten the outlook of the pessimist, the counselor brought him to a room piled high with new toys. But instead of showing delight, the little boy burst into tears. "What's the matter?" the counselor asked, baffled. "Don't you want to play with the toys?" "Yes," the little boy bawled, "but if I did, I'd only break them."

Next the counselor treated the optimist. Trying to dampen his outlook, the psychiatrist took him to a room piled to the ceiling with horse manure. But instead of wrinkling his nose in disgust, the optimist emitted a cry of delight the psychiatrist had been hoping to hear from his brother, the pessimist, when viewing the toys. The boy climbed to the top of the pile, dropped to his knees, and began enthusiastically digging out scoop after scoop with his bare hands. "What are you doing?" the psychiatrist asked, just as baffled by the optimist as he had been by the pessimist. "With all this poop," the little boy replied, beaming, "there must be a pony in here somewhere!"

We are always free to choose our attitude in any given situation, and to do that we can focus on the virtues that give us meaning and purpose. This is our soul work. Like the little optimist, we can always find the pony in the room.

"It is your attitude, more than your aptitude that will determine your altitude."

Zig Zigler, American author and speaker

Welcome Your Teachable Moments

Tests and challenges are essential for the mastery of our virtues. Resisting them out of shame or anxiety to face them only keeps us stuck or keeps the lesson in a revolving door pattern. We literally repeat the same pattern with the same results until we decide to get the point and do the inner work. Welcoming each lesson as an enthusiastic life-long learner transforms these opportunities from stressing into blessings. Even when confronted with financial or health challenges, we have the continual choice to relinquish joy and sink into despair or face life with vibrant serenity and hope.

Heather's Story: The Power of Acceptance

My friend, Heather, sent me the following email. It reveals her surprising new lifestyle that mysteriously emerged from health challenges: "We have just returned from a lovely time in Mexico. We spent seven weeks there this winter and hope to do the same next year. The warm air is so good for the bones and joints.

Life is much quieter for me these days. I am no longer on every board and committee in creation and my 'world work' is to pray and live in a more meditative space as I paint and generally enjoy the quiet. I'm in the 'be still and know' stage at the moment. That was a huge transition for me but when it happened, it did so with amazing grace and simplicity. I don't know what precipitated it, but one day it just all fell into place and I had a new life.

We bumble along with our aging bodies. We are doing pretty well, despite Jim having COPD in addition to the lingering issues after his fall. I have continuing mobility issues and use a cane all the time. But, I just go slower than I used to and we do what we can and make adjustments. I have one of those motorized stair climber gizmos so can still go up and downstairs. Thankfully, that means we can stay in our house.

I see few people these days – only as much as I really want to. I am in an Ubuntu circle singing group and love it. My soul is fed through that. I go to a monthly silent meditation and meditate at home more regularly. I water run twice a week, go to the gym twice a week and a balance class once a week so am trying to keep the mobility I still have going. Life is good!"

To me, it seems that Heather is mastering genuine acceptance and is weaving a beautiful new tapestry pattern of a more contemplative and creative life with the threads she's been given. She's a great steward of body and soul and experiences deeper contentment than ever.

The tests I endured with Post-Polio taught me to trust more deeply, both the currents of life and my relationships. I needed to rely on my husband's help and care more than ever before. I couldn't hog all the care-giving. Facing the inevitable changes of illness and aging enabled me to dive more deeply into my intuition and my creativity.

MYSTERY

"Life is not a problem to be solved, but a mystery to be lived."

Alexander Pope, 18th century English poet

All the world's sacred traditions describe a reality that goes beyond material existence, one that has to do with the realm of mystery, the experience of the sublime. If you have ever been transported by a piece of exquisite music or a spectacular sunset, that transcendent feeling lifted you beyond your everyday reality to a higher state. I believe that everyone has a deep need for a regular practice of reflection – a pause to breathe and contemplate our inner lives. We are fed by the daily bread of communion, which is essential, whether one has a clearly defined theology or not.

Inspiration literally means to "breathe in". I remember hearing Archbishop Desmond Tutu at a conference in Seattle hosted by The Dalai Lama, during which I was privileged to speak on a panel. I was blessed to be seated beside the Archbishop. The next day, he and the Dalai Lama were speaking at an "intimate" breakfast for 300 of the 80,000 who attended. I was happily seated quite near these two luminaries. The Archbishop stood at the microphone, telling us that our very lives depend on the breath of God, as he inhaled deeply, then blew gently into the mic. I was one of many transported in that moment.

Trust Your Inner Voice

Based on years of research into the world's sacred traditions as well as my own journey with prayer and meditation, I firmly believe that each of us has an "A-Team" of angels, ancestors and advisors waiting for us to ask for help. Not to do so is to promote unemployment after death! In my experience, calling on their help is a spiritual practice that brings miraculous results. This is more about opening to a greater will and seeking to serve it rather than treating the Divine like a cosmic fairy godmother, asking her to fulfill our limited, often mis-guided wishes.

Having meditated and sought the guidance of Spirit for many years, I had a remarkable experience that actually led to my being on the Oprah show. One morning as I walked out to my prayer corner in the pre-dawn light, I felt a gentle hand stop me, and heard the words, "Go to work."

"Really? Without praying first? Or even a cup of coffee?" I asked. The instructions continued.

"What do you want me to do?" I asked, now sitting at my desk in my nightie.

The inner voice clearly said, "Write to Oprah today."

The marketing department at Penguin New York had already sent out elaborate multi-page proposals to Oprah's producers about my first book, *The Family Virtues Guide*, with no response. Yet I obeyed that voice of Spirit and wrote a simple, one page proposal. A name popped into my mind – Katy Murphy. I checked online to see if she was actually with the Oprah show, and sure enough she was one of her producers. Then it occurred to me I should get permission from my editor at Penguin, so I rang her in New York.

She laughed. "It won't do you any good," she said. "You have to send it to several producers to have any chance at all. But be my guest, Linda."

So I sent my simple proposal to Ms. Murphy along with a copy of the book.

Several weeks later I was watching Oprah, and a parenting expert came on talking about managing children's behavior, saying nothing about bringing out the best in their character, nurturing their spirit, or helping them face their teachable moments, which is the focus of my book. I ranted at God. "Why did you tell me to write to Oprah if you weren't going to put me on the show?!" The next morning in my prayer corner, I humbly apologized for my outburst, and heard, "Trust My timing, dear one, not yours."

Later that day I got a call from Ms. Murphy. "I'm going to read your book. My son and I are going on holiday in Hawaii and I'll try it out with him. If it actually works, I'll pitch it to Oprah." A month later, I was sitting on camera with the icon herself, as she raved about the value of parents finally having a guide to help children become good people. During a commercial break, I asked Oprah "Would you like to hear my take on your core virtue?"

"Sure," she said.

"Reverence" I said.

"You got that right," Oprah replied. "That's why I'm the happiest girl in the USA!"

Notice Synchronicities

Norman Vincent Peale, an American minister and author known for his work in popularizing the concept of positive thinking, especially through his classic best seller, *The Power of Positive Thinking,* talked about the mystery of synchronicity. "This is a dynamic and mysterious universe and human life is, no doubt, conditioned by imponderables of which we are only dimly aware. People sometimes say, 'the strangest coincidence happened.' Coincidences may seem strange, but they are never a result of caprice. They are orderly laws in the spiritual life of man. They affect and influence our lives profoundly. These so-called imponderables are so important that you should become spiritually sensitized to them. Indeed, the more spiritually minded you become, the more acute your contact will be with these behind-the-scenes forces."

One common example is when someone suddenly comes to mind quite strongly, and soon after, you receive a call or message from them. I always say, "We crossed a thought bridge."

"Coincidence is God's way of remaining anonymous."

Albert Einstein

The RPMS of Reverence

One of the best practices to help us develop our inner life is having a daily routine of reverence. This involves creating a daily pause, to enter a sacred time of quiet, prayer or reflection. We all need a regular breathing space to contemplate what is meaningful to us. As we age, many of us become more contemplative, and require more space for solitude. Each day, we need to take sacred time, if only fifteen minutes a day, and sacred space, whether a prayer corner, a forest path, or a morning beach stroll. RPMS have to do with the efficiency of a vehicle. RPMS in a spiritual context is about spiritual efficiency, and exercising our spiritual faculties:

Read & Reflect – Read something that inspires you, whether a few lines of Scripture, a good poem, or something uplifting. Write at least a few lines in a reflection journal to track your thoughts, insights, questions and feelings.

Pray – Open yourself to inspiration. Ask for your heart's desire: ask to be of service, seek guidance on decisions that are on your mind. Record any discernment that comes, in your journal. Allow a dream to dream you.

Meditate – Prayer is the speaking part of a sacred connection. Meditation is the listening part. There are many paths to meditation, from simple breath exercises to Tai Chi, Yoga, silence, chanting a mantra, visualization, or listening for the still, small voice of wisdom. Some individuals meditate best while moving – walking, running, biking, or swimming. Others need stillness. Find your best modality. Listen deeply and trust that revelation will come.

Serve – Be open to your calling on a given day. Does someone need you to visit? Is there an idea waiting for you to give it voice? Is there a special kindness you can offer today? I often do a Virtues Pick at this point, reflecting on what virtue will guide me through the day, by randomly choosing a Virtues Card, either from a physical set of cards or by using the app on my phone. (See www.virtuesmatter.com/app) and Resources) When I have a big decision to make, I do a five-card spread, randomly choosing the Core Virtue, Guiding Virtue, Strength Virtue, Challenge Virtue and Sustaining Virtue.
www.virtuesproject.com/virtues It's amazing how fitting and illuminating these picks are.

Harvey is a lawn and landscape guy, who often comes, when no one is watching, to mow the lawn outside Hope House, the Hospice facility in our Lanai community. He told me, "I try to do something kind for someone every day. I don't give a lot of presents at Christmas. I'm a giver in the here and now. That's why they call it the present!"

"Self-rejection is the greatest enemy of the spiritual life because it contradicts the sacred voice that calls us the 'Beloved.' Being the Beloved constitutes the core truth of our existence."
Henri J.M. Nouwen, Dutch Catholic priest and author

Trust Yourself
Underlying all spiritual practice is the right relationship with the Divine, and with oneself. As we practice the presence of the sacred in our daily lives, our inner powers flourish and we have more and more freedom to dream, discern, and choose. Our intuition flowers. Without a routine of reverence, it is easy to fall under the oppressive noise and tumult of the material world and its many demands. Being open to the questions of the soul requires time. Just as in any relationship, we need regular, reliable contact. A healthy, trustworthy relationship of love and trust melts shackles and limitations that threaten our wellbeing. Above all, we need to remove whatever blocks us from knowing we are the beloved.

"Realize deeply that the present moment is all you have. Make the NOW the primary focus of your life."

Eckhart Tolle, author and spiritual teacher

Exercise 10: Practice Mindfulness

- **Take a mindful moment**

  Pause for a few minutes at least twice a day to pray, express gratitude, or to breathe deeply. Look around and notice what gives you pleasure, whether a view from your window, a color on your desk, a sensation in your body.

"The human soul needs actual beauty more than bread."

D.H. Lawrence, author

- **Expose yourself to beauty**

187

Make time in your week to listen to inspiring music, view a painting, read some beautiful words, walk through a garden, or watch waves unfurl on a beach.

- **Be fully present to your physical activitie**

I read some gorgeous words about mindfulness – being utterly present in one's body – and decided to repeat them here. What grace of language, and what a fulsome description of the holy. This is so helpful in staying out of our heads and dwelling in our deepest reality:

> *"To make bread or love, to dig in the earth, to feed an animal or cook for a stranger— these activities require no extensive commentary, no lucid theology. All they require is someone willing to bend, reach, chop, stir. Most of these tasks are so full of pleasure that there is no need to complicate things by calling them holy. And yet these are the same activities that change lives, sometimes all at once and sometimes more slowly, the way dripping water changes stone. In a world where faith is often*

construed as a way of thinking, bodily practices remind the willing that faith is a way of life." Barbara Brown Taylor, author, *An Altar in the World: A Geography of Faith*

CHAPTER ELEVEN

SUSTAIN JOY WITH GRATITUDE

"What is to come is better for you than what has gone before. For your Lord will certainly give you and you will be content...Keep recounting the favors of your Lord."

Al-Qu'ran 93

It is possible to sustain an enduring, joyful, optimistic attitude far beyond a response to passing pleasures – one that allows us to truly spread our wings. The key to sustainable joy is simple yet powerful – the practice of gratitude. As in the passage above, the sacred texts tell us that gratitude is actually a magnet for abundance, and the more thankful we are for the grace in our lives, the more grace seems to flow. Gratitude keeps us mindful of our gifts, even in trying circumstances. Gratitude helps us to be receptive to the lessons to be gleaned from our tests. It allows us to appreciate what is, and opens us to what is possible.

There are three ways to deepen our practice of gratitude, involving other companion virtues. Let go. Say yes. Give back.

LET GO

Let Go of Needless Limitations

One of the themes in this book has been the power of detachment. As we embrace a new season, we're called to release whatever blocks our physical, mental, emotional or spiritual wellbeing. We have the opportunity to shed whatever is not kind, useful, beautiful or enjoyable – whether downsizing and decluttering our homes, or finally releasing an unhealed addiction whether to a substance or a relationship. Letting go is to detach from what no longer fits the dream we choose to live now.

Whatever negative influences or beliefs have been holding us back, there's no need to continue carrying them, like outdated luggage with no wheels. If we want to be free to live authentically and meaningfully, we must unbind ourselves from attitudes that no longer serve us, false beliefs that are obstacles to being truly happy. Obstacles include other people's judgments and opinions, our own unforgiven issues, being stuck in old wounds, a sense that we aren't worthy of a great life, and dwelling on lingering guilt instead of initiating bold change.

I've been pleasantly surprised to discover that my inner sense of contentment and happiness doesn't appear to depend on being with or without illness, well off or living on a fixed income.

That being said though, actual poverty is always a fearsome reality for those who must cope with it day to day. In a just society no one should be without the essential necessities of life. It's time for all of us to wake up and learn the truth about the inequities in our world, and then act to establish justice for every soul. In my view, it's time to let go of outmoded habits of fear and dominance and open to oneness and equity. It will solve a multitude of problems.

When our basic needs for food, shelter, and safety are met – according to psychologist, Abraham Maslow's Hierarchy of Needs – happiness has more to do with giving ourselves *permission* to be happy. This is tied to self-realization, our need to be fully and freely ourselves. It is choosing to turn one's face toward the sun, opening oneself to the love of God, meaningful work, and the love and friendship of others, as willing to receive as to give. We need to realize that every behavior pattern in our relationships and every attitude is a choice. Everything is a decision.

"Expectations are pre-meditated resentments."

Alcoholics Anonymous slogan

Release Useless Pain

One of my goals in my seventh decade is to truly let go of my sense of abandonment – the oldest wound I have. It no longer holds truth. That means removing the lens with which I interpret the behavior of others who are less than loving or respectful. It also applies to the choices made by an intimate who doesn't comply with my hopes – truthfully, my expectations. Talk about cataract surgery! I am called to detach from the old familiar assumption of rejection and recognize that others' responses have more to do with them than me. The actual truth is, I have abundant love all around me, from my husband, family, and friends, and a strong sense of Divine presence. I will never be alone to face whatever comes at this season.

Many people believe that if a relationship feels hopelessly mired in negativity, boredom, or disappointment, the only way out is to walk away. From a spiritual standpoint, the path forward involves the hard work of self-examination, asking ourselves what part we are playing in the pattern. If *we* change, the dynamic of the relationship cannot remain unchanged. Expectations often consist of illusions that we can control another – a form of calcified hope. Letting go can be a powerful release. Whether we choose to walk away from a relationship, or transform it by changing the dynamic, takes deep discernment. Either way, you will be letting go of what doesn't work and moving forward with a new lens and new confidence.

"Old age is not an illness, it is a timeless ascent.

As power diminishes, we grow toward more light.

May Sarton, American poet and novelist

Let Go of Unworthiness

If we were raised by negligent, abusive or overly critical parents, we probably carry an old load of shame, a sense of not feeling worthy. This shadow can haunt us for a lifetime, unless we decide to take a long, loving look at who we have become, honor our strength virtues and fearlessly tackle our growth virtues. Any growth undertaken without shame or guilt, and instead with robust accountability and courage, will yield wondrous results. Countless individuals who seek sobriety through Alcoholics Anonymous know this journey. Others find it through a leap of faith. Transformation is always possible.

People of an advanced age often question, "Why am I still here? What purpose do I serve?" When our bodies are aging and we find ourselves having to spend more time focusing on health issues, we may experience periods of pain or fatigue. We need not interpret this as a dimming of the light. Despite our inability to navigate steps or maintain the car, or clean the house like we used to, and no matter how much time we have to spend in "doctor land", we can still engage in living with a keen sense of purpose and with confidence in our abiding worth. Sharing our stories with the young, listening to their stories without judging, offering a compassionate presence, simply smiling at people as we go about our day, are priceless gifts. Trusting our worth is essential to sustaining our joy.

Esther's Story: Unworthiness Wins

Esther, a friend of mine in her nineties, who still managed to live on her own in a lovely senior apartment, complained bitterly about being a burden to her long-suffering daughter who visited her and took her out several times a week. Having heard this complaint for years, I had finally had enough.

I said, "What if you took her help as a blessing instead of a cause for guilt? She loves doing this for you. It's her purpose. What if you were thankful instead of unhappy about it?"

She yelled back at me, "I'm completely justified in feeling guilty!"

"OK, then," I said, letting it go with as much detachment as I could muster.

A few minutes later, she said, "I just don't feel worthy, okay?"

"Now, that's insightful," I replied.

"I've never felt worthy," she said, recalling her abusive childhood and marriage. After I reminded her of all the ways she had served others during her life, and the many times she had given me

advice (we joked that I owed her a fortune in consulting fees), we agreed to disagree and went back to playing Scrabble. She beat me soundly.

SAY YES

Discover Your Yeses

"Love is yes."

Peter McWilliams, author

The Irish playwright, George Bernard Shaw, said: "This is the true joy in life, the being used for a purpose recognized by yourself as a mighty one: the being thoroughly worn out before you are thrown on the scrap heap; the being a force of nature instead of a feverish little clod of ailments and grievances complaining that the world will not devote itself to making you happy." Helen Keller, who transcended her blindness and deafness to become an inspiring author, was a force of nature. She said that rather than self-gratification, the true secret to happiness is found in "fidelity to a worthy purpose."

So, how do we stay faithful to our sense of purpose rather than giving in to the natural inclination to worry about illness, loss, being a burden, or even death? In my spiritual care work with the dying, I've seen examples of both – people who died complaining and worrying, and people who lived fully, with humor and enthusiasm to the very end. The purpose of palliative and hospice care is to help people without many days in their life to have more life in their days. Even at the end of life, we have the choice to say yes to joy or worry, gratitude or a glass eternally half full.

A volunteer driver taking me to a medical appointment told me of Eleanor, a patient she had become close to. Eleanor had recurrences of cancer in multiple sites in her body, and her prognosis was dire. Yet, said the driver, "She just sparkles."

Is it possible that we can choose to steward our own light? It's never too late to give up being a drama queen or king, to choose a path of detachment and grace. It's all a question of attitude.

Decide When to Say Yes

People often speak of how hard it is to say no, when asked to do something or participate in some volunteer activity. It's far better to reframe our choices to be about what we decide to say yes to.

Tiara's Story: Taking Her Sweet Time

Tiara, who had been working in a local shop, decided to retire when the shop was being closed because the owner wanted a smaller, more manageable business. I asked her what it felt like to be giving up her work of decades. She smiled and said, "I'm looking forward to it."

Then I asked her, "What are you going to do about all the requests you'll get to volunteer?" (I knew that on our small island, volunteers are always in great demand.)

She laughed and said, "They're already after me. I just say, 'Don't call me. I'll call you.'"

Very wise. She planned to take her time, rest her mind, and acclimate to an unpressured lifestyle here in Hawaii, before committing to a new direction. Then I asked her, "What are you looking forward to once you're free?"

"Fishing!" she said, with a huge grin.

Explore to your heart's content, and when something strikes your fancy, weave it into the tapestry of your dream lifestyle and give yourself to it, in a measure that works for you.

Say Yes Within Boundaries

Saying yes can and really should include the boundaries around your time and energy that will sustain your joy rather than turning into an unmanageable or tedious obligation. Whether a young parent, or a retiree, we need to be very aware of our energy levels. We need to recognize what drains us and what sustains us. It's time to find out what sparks our joy.

Honestly, this is true at any age. Young parents who also work outside the home have major time challenges and need to be very decisive and diligent about preserving date time with a spouse, "me time", and opportunities for occasional solitude. They are constantly giving and need to make it a priority to restore themselves regularly.

The necessity to say yes within boundaries reminds me of a teacher who did this very well. When her students begged her to hold a pizza party to celebrate the end of term, she said, "Yes. IF you raise the money to buy the pizza, your parents provide the paper plates and drinks, and one of your families chooses what pizzas to get and then picks them up." This taught the children organizational skills and gave them a serving of pride with their pizza.

So, each commitment requires some thought. Under what conditions will you retain your sense of freedom while saying yes? What would you love to do? For this reason, it's best to say, "I'll think about it" or "I'll give it a try." rather than reacting out of guilt or premature enthusiasm to the opportunities that come along. Whatever your stage of life, it's wise to always bear in mind that a pace of grace is essential to a balanced life. I recommend always getting engaged before you get "married" to a new role.

Set Holistic Goals

Saying yes to life isn't always about a search for happiness. It's better to seek wholeness, balancing body, mind and spirit. Mindfully seeking to nurture all aspects of ourselves allows us to sustain a positive attitude. While we need to accept all our emotions as they ebb and flow, we don't need to let them lead us by the nose or dominate our decisions. Reflecting on what balance feels like to you is essential. It's a form of personal time management, thoughtfully planning your exercise, your food, your service, and your fun.

Dan and I have a nightly ritual of recounting the day. It's helpful as a memory stimulant and also as a way to look at the things for which we are grateful, and the things we want to improve on the following day. At the end, Dan always asks me, "So, how was your day?" I often say, "It was balanced." I like that. For me, that means taking time for my routine of reverence, being of service in some way, time for creativity, resting proactively, and doing something pleasurable. When I'm writing, it's both work and play.

"Our calling is where our deepest gladness and the world's hunger meet."

Frederick Buechner, author and theologian

GIVE BACK

Discern Your Way to Give Back

When compassion and gratitude combine, they are a powerful antidote to anxiety and depression. Giving our love and sharing our gifts with others in a way that makes a difference ignites joy as nothing else can.

Some individuals are blessed to have a vocation –
a calling. A vocation is something that you cannot
not do! It brings a sense of joyful fulfillment.
Pleasure can be exciting and wonderful for a
moment. Service that is also a creative act is a joy
that goes on and on. Discerning our true calling
can only come with reflection on what activities
tap into the authentic expression of ourselves.
Notice what kindles your delight, your sense of
being needed, your ability to make a difference to
someone.

Parker J. Palmer, an American theologian and
author says: "Our deepest calling is to grow into
our own authentic self-hood, whether or not it
conforms to some image of who we ought to be.
As we do so, we will not only find the joy that
every human being seeks – we will also find our
path of authentic service in the world."

Ellen's Story: Turning "I wish" into "I will".

*My friend, Ellen, shared with me how she
discerned her way of giving back. She wrote: "I've
been practicing tai chi for many years and was
hoping I could reinvigorate my practice when I
moved to a new community. Unfortunately, it was
not being offered anywhere close to my home. A*

*friend who knew how much I enjoyed the practice
asked me to show some postures in one of her
classes. She informed me of an online course to
become a Tai Chi Instructor and encouraged me to
take it. Shortly after she told me about it, I
randomly picked Initiative from my set of Virtue
Cards and that got me thinking – if I really believe
in what I'm reading, I need to act. So, I did it! I
signed-up, paid the fee, followed all the lessons
and passed all the required tests until I completed
the course. This was a great personal victory for
me. I will be forever grateful to this friend and
others who have supported me, cheered me on and
directed me towards my calling even when I didn't
see it myself. In the end however it was my own
initiative that made my wishing for something into
an 'I will.' I'm as proud of that as anything."*

Saying yes to the courageous step of becoming
certified to teach others was a stretch beyond
Ellen's usual comfort zone. She has a class of
about a dozen enthusiasts, and is ecstatic about the
experience of doing something she is naturally
good at while providing a valuable community
service. Finding a purpose sourced in our deepest
enthusiasm, one that also makes a difference,
nurtures abiding joy.

Just as Ellen found tremendous joy in becoming a tai chi instructor, I absolutely love facilitating a women's circle and writing a column for the local newspaper. There is something exhilarating about using our unique talents to help others. Giving women a special forum in which to feed and support one another feeds me as well. When we meet together, our pot lucks are out of this world! We bring our best dishes. Telling our stories in an authentic way combined with Virtues Picks and acknowledgments gives us a haven of safety to be truly heard and affirmed.

Everybody has something to give. It may be that you are the visitor someone is longing to talk story with, or the organized soul who can help someone clean out their hoard of belongings, or someone who can put a smile on a child's face by simply spending time watching, listening, and playing. Every act of kindness is a form of generosity. Sharing what we have and who we are fulfills our purpose in life in priceless ways.

Jim's Story: Holy Humor

I will never forget Jim, a young man who had been wheelchair-bound as a quadriplegic since the age of eighteen when a car accident drastically changed his life. He had an amazing sense of humor and brightened my day as he probably did for countless others, including his caregivers – truly a holy purpose. The first time I saw him was at an outdoor market. An attendant was wheeling him by. Our eyes met, and I smiled. He flashed back a crooked grin. Six months later, I was in the forward lounge of a large ferry and saw him again, sitting in his wheelchair. I stopped and looked into his eyes.

"Do I know you?" he asked.

"Yes. We kind of met at the craft market."

"Oh, yeah."

I asked him, "Are you coming or going?"

He said, "I'm coming back from vegetable camp."

"What are you, a carrot?"

"No, a squash!"

The sound of our laughter turned heads. His laugh was loud, a drawing in of breath that sounded like a donkey braying. I sat down next to him. Between jokes, he told me his story. In his teens, he had had a premonition that he was going to die, and took out a life insurance policy for his single mother. Shortly afterwards, a serious car accident left him a quadriplegic. *"But I never expected this. This is harder,"* he confessed. *He went on to share his most intimate belief, that he was blessed because Jesus died for him.*

I said, "Do you realize that your sacrifice is like a small part of Jesus's pain?" His eyes glistened with unshed tears. As the ferry was pulling into the dock, I asked him what it was that gave him his good humor.

"I'm lucky," he said. "What else could happen to me?"

"Well, your hair could fall out," I said, cheekily. This time, he roared with laughter. The attendant came running and started to wheel him away.

"Wait," he said. He took my hand somehow between his, and brought it to his lips.

"I have learned to be content whatever the circumstances. I know what it is to be in need, and I know what it is to have plenty. I have learned the secret of being content in any and every situation, whether well fed or hungry, whether living in plenty or in want."

(Phillippians 4:12-13)

The Secret of a Contented Heart

The secret Paul was speaking about to the Philippians was his faith in the presence of God in all circumstances. Whatever was happening, he felt supported by abiding love. The secret also involves gratitude, a source of genuine freedom. It's been said, "It's not happiness that brings gratitude. It's gratitude that brings happiness."

The happiest people I know, who are living a dream that brings them almost constant contentment, are individuals who have learned to be grateful whatever the circumstances. An 82 year old friend locked down in the midst of a pandemic, told me "I have used the word 'grateful' more in the last few months than in my entire life altogether." When asked to share what she is grateful for, she had a list: her good health, the fact that her children still have their jobs, despite many layoffs in their profession, the fact that they can work from home, and they are paying serious attention to the guidelines about how to stay safe during Covid. She said, "This is way beyond feeling 'lucky'. I feel grateful!" I mentioned to her how good gratitude is for one's immune system.

"Oh, good, something else to be grateful for," she said.

"Gratitude is good medicine," says Robert A. Emmons, Ph.D., a professor of psychology at University of California-Davis and author of *The Little Book of Gratitude*. According to the American Heart Association, clinical trials show that the practice of gratitude has dramatic impact in a person's life. It can lower blood pressure and improve immune function. Grateful people tend to have more exercise, eat more healthily, are less likely to smoke or abuse alcohol, and also take their medications as directed. Here are some recommended steps to cultivate an attitude of gratitude:

1. Health: What did your body do for you today?
Did you know you take about eight million breaths a year? Your feet can take you on a hike. Your arms can hold someone you love. You may have recovered from an illness with amazing resilience. Take a minute to marvel at the finely tuned machinery of your body.

2. Eat: What did you feed your body to nourish yourself today?

Was it an old favorite, something you made, or something new and different? If you eat three meals a day, you'll eat about a thousand meals this year! Take a minute to savor an especially delicious meal.

3. Activity: What did you do that you really enjoyed today?

Did you give it your all to an exercise routine or take a quiet moment to reflect at the start of your day? Did you watch the sunset or gaze at the stars? Did you pause for applause after achieving a goal? Take a minute to think back on one particularly awesome moment.

4. Relationship: Who do you look forward to seeing?

Is it someone who sets your heart on fire, always has a smile for you, a friend who has your back, or someone who makes you laugh until you cry? Take a minute to smile as you think about this special person.

5. Time: What are you doing right now?

Every single day you wake up with 24 brand new hours. Take a minute to be thankful for the gift of time.

"The past is history, the future is a mystery, and today is a gift.

That's why they call it the present!"

Bil Keane, cartoonist

Being mindful of each experience, totally present and appreciative, is a goal worthy of awesome effort. When it becomes a habit and a practice, it anchors us in quiet joy. This doesn't mean becoming a monk or giving up our natural desire to strive, but it does mean having more peace in our souls as we go about our lives, and sometimes even our final days.

John's Story: Eternal Enthusiasm

My brother John was an example of gratitude and contentment as he adjusted to the new normal of a terminal illness. Having spent much of his working life in show business and as a Walt Disney Imagineer, he had constant deadlines, budgets, people and projects to manage. Most of the time he found it exhilarating. When he chose to leave that life behind to share a new dream with Dan and me as a founder of The Virtues Project, he totally enjoyed the new tempo and poured his enthusiasm into designing our books and virtues cards. When glioblastoma brain cancer came along in his early sixties, this fit, energetic man never once questioned it or asked, "Why me?" He took it as the next destination in his personal Adventureland. A week or so after his diagnosis, I found him weeping, and thought to myself, "Finally, he's facing his grief," but I was wrong.

"What are those tears, John?" I asked.

"It's so beautiful!" he said.

"What's beautiful," I asked utterly mystified.

"I've been reading the Baha'i Writings about the next world all morning, and it's just so beautiful.'

John continued to feel excited about the next phase of his journey, and one day, his oncologist said, "I've never known anyone to approach death with such peace. Why?"

John grinned and said, "Well, in our faith, prayer is communion with God, and death is reunion with God. So I can hardly wait. And I've always loved change!" Our brother, John's twin, Tommy and I cried silently while John just beamed.

Always a man of humor, he had a whole new set of witty remarks about death. When people asked him how he was doing, he'd say, with a laugh, "I'm way past my sell-by date." When he was hospitalized, he'd cheerily greet the nurse coming to give him a shot: "Oh, are you here for my grab and stab?"

This man, who served as Design Director for Tokyo Disney for six years, got to the point where he couldn't find the "on" button on the coffee pot, couldn't walk without a walker, and could barely feed himself. Yet he would say, "You know, Lin, this isn't an emergency. It's an emergence." After a final seizure, he went into hospice for one night and some friends came to see him. As they stood around his bed, he was semi-conscious, but when a friend said, "I was going to make you a blueberry pie, John." "Was?!" he said suddenly with irony and humor, and we all laughed. He died the next day.

John is my model for how to make the most and the best out of any circumstances. I need to nurse and acknowledge my sadness, grief, and disappointments for a while, before I can transform them into acceptance and contentment. There's no one path to get there, but joy is always waiting if we're willing to turn the mirror of our hearts toward it.

"God grant me the Serenity to accept the things I cannot change; Courage to change the things I can; and the Wisdom to know the difference."

Prayer by Reinardt Niebuhr, used in Alcoholics Anonymous 12 Step programs

Reflection Exercise 11: Nurture Your Joy and Gratitude

- Letting Go: In a journal, divide a page in half and list on the left side the things you want to let go of, and want less of at this time in your life.

- Saying Yes: On the right side, across from each item, write the practice or virtue that will replace these old situations: for example, replace worry with trust; negative self-talk with virtues corrections. Replace "I'm such a chronic worry wart" with "I deepen my practice of trust." (See Virtues List at www.virtuesproject.com/virtues)

- Reflect on and journal the boundaries that will guide and protect your time, energy and wellbeing. Be specific. For example, "I will only take on two volunteer activities this year." Or "I will only seek work that ignites my joy."

- Explore and brainstorm activities that give you joy, and say yes to pursuing them actively.

- Giving Back: With your particular gifts in mind, choose a way to contribute. Discover your authentic service, your calling.

- Practice gratitude: Court contentment by keeping a gratitude journal, counting your blessings each morning and before bed. What were you most grateful for today?

CHAPTER TWELVE
GET SET FOR YOUR LEAP OF FAITH

"If I were to wish for anything, I should not wish for wealth and power, but for the passionate sense of the potential,
for the eye which, ever young and ardent, sees the possible."
Soren Kierkegaard, Danish philosopher

"A leap of faith" is an expression coined by Soren Kierkegaard. It describes moving beyond logic and reason alone into a relationship of faith with the unknowable Divine. It's the perfect phrase for this stage of the dreaming process – actually stepping off the known path into your dream of the possible.

Throughout this book, we have been exploring ways to tap into your inner vision, your intuitive, perceptive knowing of what you are drawn to at a crossroads of change. Whatever the circumstances, virtues are your guideposts – your love, your enthusiasm, your creativity, your wisdom, your sense of wonder, your compassion.

It may be useful to gather the threads woven through *Dreaming* which have been a preparation process for moving forward at this season of your life. The provisions for your journey are your virtues practices – your spiritual strengths.

1: Find the Courage to Choose Change

Decide to decide. Whether forced into change by unforeseen events, changing circumstances, or by your own boredom with the way things are, venture to step out of your comfort zone and contemplate the choices before you. Dare to discern. Tell the truth and accept the things you cannot change. Even within the most seemingly limited circumstances, there are many paths you could take, if you call on your courage.

2: Face Grief and Loss as a Catalyst for Hope

Allow yourself to grieve what you are giving up or what you have lost. Grieving is a healthy necessity, and when fully experienced, serves as a catalyst for hope. Dwelling in vague sorrow and depression dampens hope for the future. Honoring our deepest sadness by getting to the heart of the matter clears the way for a new dream to take shape. Saying goodbye to the old is as important as saying hello to the new. Get the support you need to navigate your grief.

> *"The breezes at dawn have secrets to tell you. Don't go back to sleep!*
> *You must ask for what you really want. Don't go back to sleep!"*
> Jalal u Din Rumi, Sufi poet

3: Trust the Process

You don't have to have a complete plan in advance, but only a plan for transition – a starting point, with a landing place to begin exploring. Trust your own unknowing. Trust the currents of Grace.

Jan Garrett's exquisite song, *Don't Go Back to Sleep* is based on Rumi's poem. The lyrics include these words:

You know that you must ask for your treasure
Move, therefore, toward the greatest pleasure
Fight to stay awake
Choose the path you take
Even if you don't know where it's going
Trust your own unknowing
Don't go back to sleep

Ruth's Story: Daring to Leap

Ruth was a dedicated teacher for years. She had been divorced for several years and was longing for a full partner, one who would share her passions and her faith. She was a devout Christian and had a calling to make a difference in the world in a new way. She felt strongly that her years of teaching needed to come to an end, and wanted to pursue her calling wherever it might take her. She had no clear idea of what that would look like. She consulted me about keeping her rented apartment in the town where she had been living for a decade "in case" things didn't work out and she would need to retreat back to her known life. What swiftly came to mind was Jesus's words to his disciples: "When you depart out of that house or city, shake off the dust of your feet." (Mathew 10:14) Ruth had substantial savings, excellent skills, a passion for service, and three friends who welcomed her to stay with them in other parts of the world to which she was attracted. She decided to sell her car, release her belongings and fly, trusting in her own unknowing. Holding on to the past with one hand while attempting to fly in a new direction may well disrupt one's flight pattern.

"Sometimes taking a leap of faith requires an imaginative mind that can create the ending you are unable to see."
Shannon L. Alder, author and therapist

4: Dare to Dream

Be willing to discover your passion and pleasures. Find a new path that ignites your joy. What really lights you up? You can see the sudden radiance on the faces of people talking about something that they really love to do. You're likely to find that it has an element of service or giving back, since that brings genuine soul satisfaction. Discerning what you really want and identifying your yeses is essential to sustain your wellbeing as you take a new direction.

5: Set Your House in Order

Let go literally and emotionally of the things that no longer fit you, whether remnants of early wounding, a long dysfunctional relationship, or clothes that don't fit the lifestyle that you're ready to create. Cleansing and purifying your space is a powerful way to release long held guilt about procrastination and all the undone things. Creating a new sense of order invites the virtue of clarity, bringing lucidity of thought and purity of intention. What you truly value may well emerge as you clean and clear.

"Letting go gives us freedom, and freedom is the only condition for happiness.
If, in our heart, we still cling to anything – anger, anxiety, or possessions –
we cannot be free."
Thich Nhat Hanh, Buddhist monk

6: Enter Your Freedom Season

Strengthen your detachment muscle. Free yourself from limited thinking, fear-based clinging, and old habits and addictions that hold you back from your best life. Step away from the pain you have needlessly carried and open yourself to new life.

7: Be Independently Wealthy

Reevaluate your relationship with material things, and with money. Define what *you* really treasure, not what the world says that you should be doing or acquiring in order to be "successful." Define success by what makes you whole and satisfies your soul.

Court contentment and live more lightly on the land. The very air we breathe is at risk unless the consumerist culture that attempts to control us through countless media messages is resisted in the name of independence. Share more, hoard less. True wealth is found not by what we keep but by what we give.

8: Create New Boundaries

As you discern what you value, including your freedom to play with possibilities as long as you choose, set your personal boundaries around your energy, time and commitments. Get engaged with an activity before you get married to it. Only make promises that you genuinely want to keep and to which you can honestly and happily invest yourself. Consider what comforts you need before rushing off to a jungle, a desert or an unknown city. As we age, comfort is queen! It enables us to give our best. Reset your relationships, including with grown children. New patterns are called for, as you leave the role of caregiver and take on the role of mentor and friend, respecting their right to make their own life choices.

9: Play is the New Work

Learn how to play in a way that brings joy at your particular season. Explore, connect, create. Play with children, being fully present to their way of seeing the world. Have fun! If your work and your play are indistinguishable, you are truly blessed. Play with possibilities for solving the inevitable challenges of life. Invite others to imagine with you.

"Spirituality is not a formula; it is not a test. It is a relationship.

Spirituality is not about competency; it is about intimacy.

Spirituality is not about perfection; it is about connection.

The way of the spiritual life begins where we are now

in the mess of our lives."

Mike Yaconelli, author

10: Cultivate Your Spirituality

Spirituality is not about being perfect or unreal. It is about encountering the sacred right in the midst of our messy lives. Connecting with our soul qualities of love, justice, hope, purposefulness, kindness, compassion, forgiveness, creativity and joy, is indeed the *most* real and authentic way to live. To understand the "anatomy" of spirituality, it's helpful to reflect on three elements: meaning, mastery and mystery. What makes life meaningfu for you? What purpose calls to you that will make your time as fulfilling as possible? It won't be some idealized life. It will be what *you* need to sink your teeth into. It will be your taste – your truth – that determines your dream.

Whatever path you choose, consciously cultivate your spiritual powers. Develop mastery little by little, day by day, responding humbly and enthusiastically to the lessons in your tests – your teachable moments. This is the most spiritually efficient way to live the richest life possible.

Open yourself to mystery, through the beauty of nature, enjoying the arts, deepening your prayer life, honing your meditative skills, or contemplating life from a spiritual perspective. What is your relationship like with your Higher Power? Intimacy with God is closely linked to intimacy with yourself. Establish a daily routine o reverence, creating sacred time and space to do your RPMS. Read, Pray, Meditate, Serve. Include Virtues Picks in your practice as it helps to deepen your mindfulness of these powerful qualities within you. Listening to your inner wisdom and acting on its guidance opens new worlds before you. It is the essence of self-actualization.

11: Sustain Joy with Gratitude

The virtue that most amply supports us to sustain joy is gratitude. Gratitude is conducive to bounty. It magnetizes abundance and wellbeing. Consciously counting our blessings, being deeply aware of our gifts, including and especially in troubling times, brings transcendence. Three aspects of the practice of gratitude are letting go of negativity in any form. That doesn't mean denial of our sense of righteous indignation in the face of injustice. It means finding a positive way forward in any situation, letting go of limitations that hold us back, whether doubt, fear, or lack of self-confidence. Second, gratitude grows as we say yes to what really resonates for us at this season. It's far more meaningful to discern what you want to say yes to than focusing on saying no to the demands of others. What is your portal to express your love and to receive love? What is your joy?

Finally, give back. It is only in our contribution that our highest freedom and greatest joy can be found. Gratitude impels us to be givers.

"We must be willing to let go of the life we have planned,

so as to have the life that is waiting for us."

E. M. Forster, author

Time to Commit to Your Leap of Faith
As you stand at the crossroads of your life, having prepared yourself for the dream that may well be your destiny or your delight at this season, you find yourself at the moment of truth. It's time to act. As you act, courageously taking each next right step, all kinds of things you could not have anticipated will unfold and flower before you. Scottish mountaineer and author W.H. Murray, recalling words by Goethe, said: "Concerning all acts of initiative (and creation) there is one elementary truth, the ignorance of which kills countless ideas and splendid plans: that the moment one definitely commits oneself, then providence moves too. All sorts of things occur to help one that would not otherwise have occurred." There is a definite ripple effect in the energy of the

universe when we make a commitment. The more you trust rather than clinging to the past or even the known, the more energy you radiate in your leap of faith.

Reflection Exercise 12:

- Call on your imagination to define your vision. Be very alert to synchronicities and inner guidance as you write it out. Describe it in present tense "I am, I have, I do." Let your mind open fully to how you envision a new way forward.

- Make a detailed plan for how you will initiate your decision. An effective way to plan is to think in terms of three months. Set goals, but only a few that you can keep in focus. In the next three months, what actions will you take to fulfill your goals? Write them in a circular fashion, clockwise with the name of your vision in the center and a virtue that will support you to achieve it. Write 3 to 5 goals with the steps or tactics for each below. Illustrate it, color it, or collage it. In some way, make it come alive. Your mind responds energetically when you set a clear course for yourself, even when you can't see the twists and turns ahead.

CHAPTER THIRTEEN
FOLLOW YOUR DREAM

"To everything there is a season, and a time for every purpose under heaven."
Ecclesiastes 3:1

Standing at the crossroads of change, we naturally face the unknown. We don't really know what lies ahead on the road we have chosen. We will never know where the "other" road would have taken us. Taking time to explore the possibilities and discern a way forward, detecting what really calls to us at this season, is ideal. Yet, life doesn't always happen that way.

Trust Your Own Unknowing
There are times when circumstances shift very quickly, and decisiveness calls us to make a choice swiftly, without hesitation, prompted by an intuitive sense that it is right and timely. Not every crossroads allows us the luxury of a long discernment process. However, even in the midst of a change of seasons that seems rapid and compelling, we must hold our decision lightly, open to the clarity that will come. Once

we determine the road we want to take, each move in that direction occurs one step at a time. All we need to do is to focus mindfully on that single next step. It's like stepping onto a dance floor, trusting our body to know how to move. Trust is a huge component of discerning when to wait and when to move quickly.

One day, when we were still living in Aitutaki, our hairstylist (the best I've ever had) came to our home to give Dan and me haircuts. She mentioned some shocking news. One of the American expats on the island, who had been there for a couple of decades, was told as he reentered the Cook Islands after a trip to the States, that new immigration rules only allowed him to stay for three months at a time. This meant he had to leave the country four times a year, applying for a visa each time at the cost of a hefty fee, not to mention the travel costs. This man was deeply embedded in the community, had built a house near the beach, and had close friends. The rules did not apply to individuals who had been granted permanent residence status, but that privilege was indefinitely suspended. We had a trip to the U.S. scheduled three weeks hence, but this shocking news felt like a flashing warning light that suddenly changed our reality. We expected to be in the Cook Islands for the rest of our lives and even had our burial sites secured on the land of close friends, who were like family.

I immediately called Immigration to verify the information, only to discover that it was true! I had secured a work permit as a columnist for Cook Islands News, so thought I might be exempt, but was told that it would not be renewed. Dan and I are not ones to disobey the laws of the land, however arbitrary they might seem. We consulted together and prayed. Dan suggested that if we had to leave, we should go to Hawaii, so that we could stay connected to Polynesian culture and island life – our possible Step One. Our process for decisions as a couple is for Dan to observe the patterns and follow them to logical resolution. Mine was to seek guidance through prayer and meditation. When the two converge, we act.

Dan said, "You'd better meditate and ask for guidance," but my mind was reeling. Each day for the next three days, I went into my sanctuary, the room where I prayed, wrote, and kept my library, and tried to calm down enough to meditate. Each day I asked for clarity and guidance, and Dan would ask what came to me. On the third day, clarity came. I went into a visual meditation where I saw my advisors in a circle, as I often had in the past. They include souls in the spiritual realm that have come into my awareness over the years, including my father. In the center of the circle, I saw a Hawaiian island with high green mountains, and heard a voice saying, "Linda, we need you. We really need you." After sharing this with Dan, I then took the next step, to find the national Baha'i community of Hawaii online and wrote an email, asking if we could be of service. Surprisingly, I received an instant response. A woman I had never met, but who had heard of us and our work with The Virtues Project, responded, "Linda, we need you. We really need you." When something I receive inwardly coincides with something outside my control, I pay attention, and take it as a confirmation. Her email contained the exact words I had heard in meditation.

We decided to act quickly, and to make the upcoming departure our final one. The disruption and expense of departing every three months at the cost of thousands of dollars in airfare alone was impossible for us.

After tearful goodbyes to our family and friends at the airport, we boarded the plane for the short flight to Rarotonga to connect with the international flight to LAX. I couldn't stop crying. We were met in Raro by a group of friends, including a former pastor who had become like a brother to me when he worked as a school counselor on Aitutaki. We met weekly to pray, share our spiritual insights and talk about virtues strategies to help his young clients. He pulled me aside. "Linda, I need to tell you something. Two years ago when we had one of our sessions together, I heard God say, 'She won't be here long. She's going to Hawaii.' I just looked it up in my journal. And one of you is going to need medical care." Talk about mystery!

Our next step was to choose which island to live on. We had asked the National Spiritual Assembly of the Baha'is of Hawaii which island needed our help. They named three, Lanai being the smallest. So, we chose Lanai as our landing place. We were welcomed warmly by the local Baha'is and even given a home to stay in while we discerned if we could indeed settle there. We were prepared to move on to one of the other islands and did research on all of them, yet we felt drawn to Lanai. We decided to stay. There was one obstacle – housing was incredibly tight. Yet, despite long waiting lists for rental apartments, we found that the sea of opportunity parted for us and we were assigned one quickly. People kept asking, "How did you get in so fast?" I would just shrug and point up.

Lanai truly feels like home. For us at this season, a quiet rural atmosphere of natural beauty and an ethnically diverse community is most appealing. As it turns out, I did need serious medical care in the form of open heart surgery, which would not have been possible on our beloved Aitutaki. My friend's prophecy was indeed accurate.

In hindsight it looks as though we were simply carried on a wave of Grace, yet I needed to hold tightly to my courage, resilience, and above all trust, in order to navigate the waves of this change, including my grief. My brother, John, would have called it taking Vitamin T – trust.

> *"You see things; and you say, 'Why?' But I dream things that never were; and I say, 'Why not?'"*.
> George Bernard Shaw, Irish playright

Reflection Exercise 13: Lean into Courage

Some people have a rocky relationship with decisiveness. They spend agonizing months, even years, trying to figure out all the "what ifs" before choosing a path forward. This painful process is often a form of spiritual procrastination – a slow, indecisive meandering in circles, which causes them ongoing anxiety. Tearing off the bandage of one's known life quickly seems much less painful, clearing the way for the adventure ahead.

- Tell the truth: Dare to dream big, while recognizing the realistic boundaries of your resources – your time, money, health requirements, family preferences and especially your own heart's desires.

- Know yourself: Discern your deepest values. What and who do you need to populate a

235

rich life? Is it natural beauty, more access to city life, adventure, travel, creativity, or service that calls most deeply to you?

- Reflect: Tap into your own way of seeking guidance and give it your full attention.

- Act decisively. Once you have followed steps such as those in this book, go for it! A the Nike motto goes, Just DO It! Trust that you will make adjustments in a way that works for you.

- Appreciate your assets and all that comes to you along the road. Throughout any journey we can be thankful for what is being given to us, or constantly bemoan what we have lost. Every path has its losses, wonders and gifts.

- Accept your own choice without secon guessing yourself. You always have th right to change your mind if you find tha this path isn't really the one that fits you life. You can always modify your choices i creative ways. At the very least you will learn what works for you and what doesn't. In this sense, there really is no failure, only life unfolding.

CHAPTER FOURTEEN
DREAMING A NEW WORLD

"We are not going to be able to operate our spaceship earth successfully nor for much longer unless we see it as a whole spaceship and our fate as common. It has to be everybody or nobody."
R. Buckminster Fuller, author and futurist

We've been exploring the journey to discern a personal dream, a path through change to a life more in alignment with your values and ideals. Many believe, as do I, that humanity is at a crossroads as well.

New light is being shed on how the health of all of us is bound with the health of the poorest among us, and the powerful lens of our electronics has catalyzed an intimate empathy for those suffering injustice and racial hatred for generations.

The ills of the world and the critical need for change are right before our eyes as never before. It can be overwhelming. Yet, there is a growing passion to burst out of our helplessness, to follow what the young environmentalist, Greta Thunberg says, confronting those in power: "Right here, right now is where we draw the line. The world is waking up. And change is coming whether you like it or not." In one of her most stinging speeches, this small slender sixteen year old told world leaders at the United Nations General Assembly that future generations won't let them get away with their lack of action against climate change. "Together and united, we are unstoppable."

Our very survival is entwined with that of the earth on which we breathe, move, and have our being. Films such as David Attenborough's 2020 "A Life on Our Planet" reveals the beauty of a biodiversity we literally cannot afford to lose. The Netflix documentary, "Kiss the Earth" unpacks the ways in which the earth's soil may be the key to combatting climate change and preserving the planet. The film reveals the first viable solution to our climate crisis, showing that, by regenerating the world's soils, we can completely and rapidly stabilize Earth's climate, restore lost ecosystems and create abundant food supplies.

There are glimmerings of hope for a new dream – a world beyond prejudice, poverty, and injustice, a world where black lives matter and human life matters more than greed, where success is no longer narrowly measured by the Gross National Product, but by health, equity and the wellbeing of people. During the Covid pandemic, a handwritten sign on a piece of plywood boarding up a closed shop in Maui, Hawaii read: "Are we really waiting for a return to normal or are we ready to build something different?" (Eliana Levy)

Bucky Fuller offered much wisdom to those seeking a hopeful world view. One of his sayings that resonates for me is, "Think globally. Act locally." What would that look like for each of us? I sincerely believe it is time for us to come out of the numbing denial of our collective sins against one another and the planet and do our part for what New York Times columnist and author, David Brooks calls "The Great Reset" – a consciousness that has spread rapidly like a cleansing flood across the world.

"We know that we are the ones who are divided
and we are the ones who must come back together
to walk in the sacred way."
Ojibway Prayer

Cross the Divide

What if we dare to dream of a unity that crosses all barriers? In our divided world, it may seem we are staring across an impossible chasm in our ways of thinking and our politics. Yet, we stand on common ground when it comes to our humanness. I don't believe it is an exaggeration to say that as each of us finds a path to peace with those who seem "other", we are sending out ripples that can eventuate in world peace.

Encountering someone who sees the world differently and would probably scoff at the words written here, the key to peace is to *get curious, not furious*. Ask questions and listen mindfully. Choose to use positive inquiry to learn and understand a different, even opposite perspective. "I see it quite differently. Help me understand how you see it." Those three words – help me understand – are disarming. For most of us, I think it's important to engage *only* in civil discourse, refusing to add fuel to the fires of disunity.

After a long listen to a friend who sees the world in a way that from my perspective seems black and white rather than full of color, rigid rather than open, and full of passionately held misinformation, my only comment was "Thank you for your clarity in explaining this to me. I can see that you're truly a righteous person." I was a bit sad that the same curiosity wasn't extended to me, but left the encounter genuinely enlightened, no longer puzzled about "How can they think like that?!" I could actually understand this contained belief system. While I refuse to engage in conflict, I do believe in speaking my truth, so, I did say a few words from my viewpoint about the importance o racial equity and climate change, as well as the importance of fact checking, which met with a glazed expression and no further interest.

Civil discourse doesn't prevent us from sharing the truth as we see it. The truth really does set us free. I made a commitment many years ago, and for the most part have kept it, never to collude with racism or ethnic prejudice in my presence. When someone makes a slur or generalization in my company, I immediately speak up with both tact and conviction (using the Language of Virtues) to say, "That isn't my experience. To me, a fair way to see it is…" Or "We can't really generalize about people. They're all individuals. It's important to respect that." Or "Those disrespectful words don't serve you well. Please use respectful language."

Most important of all, cross the divide of ignorance. Take a humble posture of learning about the issues of the day, including racism, whatever your race may be. Systemic racism affects all of us. The great activist, Angela Davis said, "In a racist society it is not enough to be non-racist, we must be anti-racist." A quotation from an unknown source says, "Equal rights for others does not mean less rights for you. It's not pie." There is much work to be done in our varying societies around the world to establish justice, to hold those in power accountable. Locally, we are all influencers over public policy, if we choose to be. Yet, perhaps the greatest impact comes from our personal integrity to stand up and speak up as a voice for justice.

Walk your Talk

There are good reasons to be unapologetic idealists, especially if we are willing to sacrifice or modify outmoded habits – the ways we eat, shop, spend, think and legislate.

Be an advocate for positive change. Be willing to engage in piercing the veils of ignorance and seeking the truth about the dream desperately needed for a new world. There is a cost involved. We have to be willing to endure some discomfort. Learning about the devastating effects of the carbon footprint each of us leaves on the earth can be very uncomfortable. Learning about systemic racism is deeply disturbing.

The Netlflix documentary, "13th," directed by Ava du Vernay, is titled after the Thirteenth Amendment to the United States Constitution, adopted in 1865, which abolished slavery throughout the United States and ended involuntary servitude except as a punishment for conviction of a crime. It reveals how the U.S. prison system continues to perpetuate slavery through mass incarceration and exploitation of black men. After I watched it, I dissolved in sobs. I had brought The Virtues Project to prisons across North America and the world, without knowing a thing about this. My own ignorance felt like a betrayal. Yet, those cleansing tears were well worth the educating of my soul.

A great example of a business leader walking his talk is Hamdi Ulukayam, the CEO of Chobani Yogurt. He took a failing business and rebuilt it based on his conviction that people matter more than profits. In an illuminating Ted talk, he mentioned virtues such as nobility, joy, dignity, gratitude, and service to the community. He honors his employees with profit-sharing, and built a Little League baseball field in a town where one of his factories is located. He makes decisions about products based on environmental impact. Ulukayam walks his talk about what he values, putting profit in its place, doing well by doing good. Chobani has become #1 in yogurt sales.

Be Hopeful
To be a part of the quiet revolution for positive change moving in waves across our world, we need to hold onto hope. Our optimism itself is a thought force that creates more of a ripple effect than we can imagine.

It's encouraging to learn that there are many small and large movements across the world, as well as individuals making a huge difference. One of my heroes is Peace Pilgrim – Mildred Lisette Norman – an American spiritual teacher, mystic, pacifist, vegetarian activist and peace activist. In 1952, she became the first woman to walk the entire length of the Appalachian Trail in one season. Starting on

January 1, 1953, in Pasadena, California, she adopted the name "Peace Pilgrim" and walked across the United States for 28 years, speaking with others about peace. She was on her seventh cross-country journey when she died. She said, "If we knew how powerful our thoughts were, we would never again have another negative thought."

"Nothing is impossible. The word itself says 'I'm possible'!"
Audrey Hepburn, actress

Be a Unifier
One of the things that changes the world is when like-minded individuals come together to collaborate, using the creative power of their diverse viewpoints to reveal new solutions. We've talked about the value of calling a mastermind circle to brainstorm the path ahead for us as individuals. There is nothing we cannot solve if we come together in wider circles to consult on transformational ways forward.

Here is a passage from a blogpost series I co-authored with Dave Feldman, co-founder with Dara Feldman of Virtues Matter, entitled "A

Whole New World: 7 Virtues for the Great Reset."
It concerns an initiative to transform the values of
governance, departing from the long held
assumption that the gross national product of a
country defines its power and success, and instead
focusing on what will actually benefit human
beings:

> "Unity leads to humane and innovative
> decisions in governance. Three national
> leaders have united in a new network to
> develop "an alternative future based on well-
> being and inclusive growth." The three
> women leading Scotland, Iceland, and New
> Zealand are redefining national success by
> prioritizing sustainability, mental health and
> family time over the obsession with GNP as
> the only measure of prosperity. Nicola
> Sturgeon of Scotland gave a brilliant Ted
> talk about this."

So many of us ask at some point, what can I do?
Reach out to others who are of a different color, or
culture, or way of thinking, whether it be in person
or online. Befriend them. Develop a personal
connection. Feed one another with unfamiliar
dishes and ideas. Our travels in the world have

brought us astonishing gifts of intimacy with people utterly different from us in external ways, yet we are now closely bound together with trust, faithfulness and abiding love. We are family.

We need to come together to heal our world, with inclusiveness, common purpose, and collaboration. An African proverb says, "If you want to go fast, go alone. If you want to go far, go together."

> *"ain't yet no word for a world without children starved and lonesome...*
> *ain't yet no word for a world where each mistake is a holy possibility to improve...*
> *ain't yet no word for a world with no fear.*
> *ain't yet.*
> *but we working."*
> Excerpts from *what it is & will be,* in **Finna**, by poet Nate Marshall

There are only holy possibilities before us. May you find your joy, your place, your calling, and create a life that is truly an authentic expression of you at this season.

AFTERWORD

There have been many disruptions to the writing of this book – illness, the move from Aitutaki, Cook Islands to Lanai, Hawaii, and a period of grief as I mourned the loss of the place and people with whom I expected to live out my days. Yet, I relish the wonders and beauty of life on our new island home, with multiple services for seniors, superior medical care, cooler breezes, and fabulous people of spirit, intelligence, and warmth, some of whom, within a year, have become close friends. This change has given me fertile ground for my own dreaming. I've come full circle to once again serve in spiritual care and bereavement at a hospice, and am still a writer in Paradise, with plenty of time for my craft.

I sincerely hope that this book has been a catalyst for your dreaming. I would so appreciate your generosity to write a few words of review on Amazon. Take good care of your precious self, and may joy give you wings at this season.

ACKNOWLEDGMENTS

I'm thankful to the Lanai Writers' Circle – poet Christo Andrus, pharmacist cum writer, Kert Shuster, and author Linda Orvis, for their insightful and encouraging comments on *Dreaming*. A special shout out to Linda for her generosity of time and her eagle eye in providing a final edit of *Dreaming*, while writing her own book, *The Fight for Life*. Bless my alpha readers, for your honest and discerning feedback: Alberta DeJetley, Nelinia Cabiles, Evelyn Belzer, David Feldman, Morgan Brooks, and my brother, Tommy Kavelin. A heart full of gratitude to Dan – my partner in all our spiritual adventures, leaps of faith, and island hops – who trusts and nurtures all my dreams for change.

ABOUT THE AUTHOR

Linda Kavelin-Popov is a best-selling author whose books have been translated into more than a dozen languages. She has traveled the world for decades as an international speaker on personal and global transformation. Linda is the co-founder with her husband, Dr. Dan Popov and late brother, John Kavelin, of The Virtues Project, a global initiative that inspires the practice of virtues in everyday life. The Project, founded in 1991, has sparked a global revolution of kindness, justice, and integrity in more than 120 countries. It was honored by the United Nations as a "model global program for families of all cultures," and endorsed by The Dalai Lama. Linda was named a "cultural creative" by Time Magazine. She appeared on Oprah debuting her first book, *The Family Virtues Guide,* and had her own television series on Vision TV in Canada, "Virtues: A Family Affair." As a psychotherapist, she designed suicide and violence prevention programs used in U.S. mental health clinics. She is also a hospice spiritual care counselor. *Dreaming at the Crossroads of Change* is Linda's seventh book. She has two sons and seven grandchildren scattered around the planet, and now lives on Lanai, Hawaii with her husband.

OTHER BOOKS BY LINDA KAVELIN-POPOV

The Family Virtues Guide: Simple Ways to Bring Out the Best in Our Children and Ourselves

Sacred Moments: Daily Meditations on the Virtues

The Virtues Project Educators' Guide: Simple Ways to Create a Culture of Character

A Pace of Grace: the Virtues of a Sustainable Life

Graceful Endings: Navigating the Journey of Loss and Grief

A novel: *The Scent of Sage*

Linda is also the author of the *Virtues Cards* for families, classrooms, and personal spiritual practice, including cards for seventeen different Faiths. The Resilience Cards set (also known as Sunset Meditations) show sunset photos on Aitutaki taken by Dr. Dan Popov.

RESOURCES

Blog series by Linda Kavelin-Popov and Dave Feldman: "A Whole New World: 7 Virtues for the Great Reset" www.virtuesmatter.com/blog

Download the Virtues Cards app:
www.virtuesmatter.com/app

Linda's author website and blog:
www.lindakavelinpopov.com

Information on The Virtues Project:
www.virtuesproject.com

Virtues books and materials at Amazon
www.amazon.com and www.virtuesshop.com

List of 100 Virtues:
https://www.virtuesproject.com/virtuesdef.html

Five Virtues Strategies:
https://www.virtuesproject.com/Pdf/5VirtuesStrategies.pdf

Speak the Language of Virtues:
https://www.virtuesproject.com/Pdf/SpeaktheLan
uage.pdf

Offer Spiritual Companioning:
https://www.virtuesproject.com/Pdf/OfferCompar
ng.pdf

BIBLIOGRAPHY
Some of the Books & Films referenced in
Dreaming at the Crossroads

Condo, Marie, *The Life-Changing Magic of Tidying Up*

DeAngelo, Robin, *White Fragility*

Emmons, Robert A., Ph.D., *The Little Book of Gratitude*

Gillies, Jerry, *The Money Love Manifesto*
Kidd, Sue Monk, *When the Heart Waits* and other books

Marshall, Nate, *Finna*

Morgenstern, Julie, *Organizing from the Inside Out*

Palmer, Parker J. *On the Brink of Everything:* Grace, Gravity, and Getting Old and other books

Peale, Norman Vincent, *The Power of Positive Thinking*

Pipher, Mary, *Women Rowing North*

Ruiz, Don Miguel, *The Four Agreements*

Taylor, Barbara Brown Taylor, *An Altar in the World:* A Geography of Faith

Thunburg, Greta, *No One is Too Small to Make a Difference*

Thunburg, Greta et al *Our House is on Fire*

Twist, Lynne, *The Soul of Money*

Films
Attenborough, David, *A Life on Our Planet*

Du Vernay, Ava, *13th*, a Netflix documentary

Just Mercy based on the book by Bryan Stevenson

Kiss the Earth, a Netflix documentary, narrated by Woody Harrelson

The Social Dilemma, a Netflix documentary

Made in the USA
Las Vegas, NV
31 July 2023

75478013R00144